ESOTERIC RELIGIOUS STUDIES SERIES

Book#15

NATIVE AMERICAN
Spirituality and Vision Quests

Esoteric Religious Studies Series
NATIVE AMERICAN
SPIRITUALITY AND VISION QUESTS

Author: Diohka Aesden
Publisher: Cineris Multifacet
Publication Date: 2023
ISBN: - 9798874422165

For inquiries and permissions, please contact:
Cineris Multifacet
cinerismultifacet@gmail.com

Design and Typesetting:
Cineris Multifacet

Cover Design:
Cineris Multifacet

Disclaimer:

Manufactured in the United States of America

First Edition: 2023

ISBN-13: - 9798874422165

19   54   95

This page left intentionally blank.

OTHER BOOKS IN THIS SERIES

A WORLD OF ESOTERIC THOUGHT

ESOTERIC RELIGIOUS STUDIES SERIES

NATIVE AMERICAN
SPIRITUALITY AND VISION
QUESTS

Dedicated to

the Seven Campfires

and to

Pope Philo III

A

ALPHA

May the reader of the **Esoteric Religious Studies Series** be blessed abundantly. We extend our heartfelt gratitude for your engagement with this sagacious study of esoteric traditions. As you adventure through the pages, may your mind be illuminated with knowledge and your heart be filled with *wisdom*. May the insights and revelations within these texts expand your understanding and bring clarity to your spiritual path. May you be well-informed, enriched, and guided by the sacred *wisdom* that unfolds before you. May this series be a source of encouragement, transformation, and blessings upon your life.

If you enjoy the words of this book, please respect leaving a review in the marketplace you found it so that its content can reach even more interested individuals.

Please visit the author page of Diohka Aesden to keep up with new releases on religion, esoterica, mythology, and other related topics.

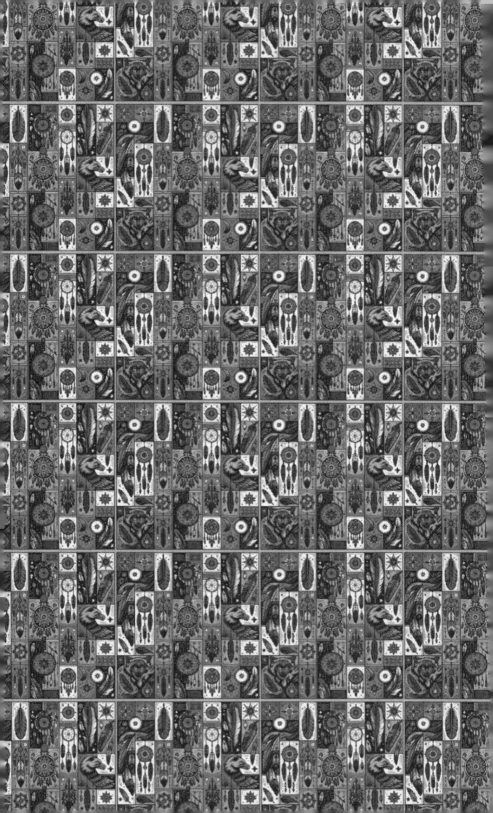

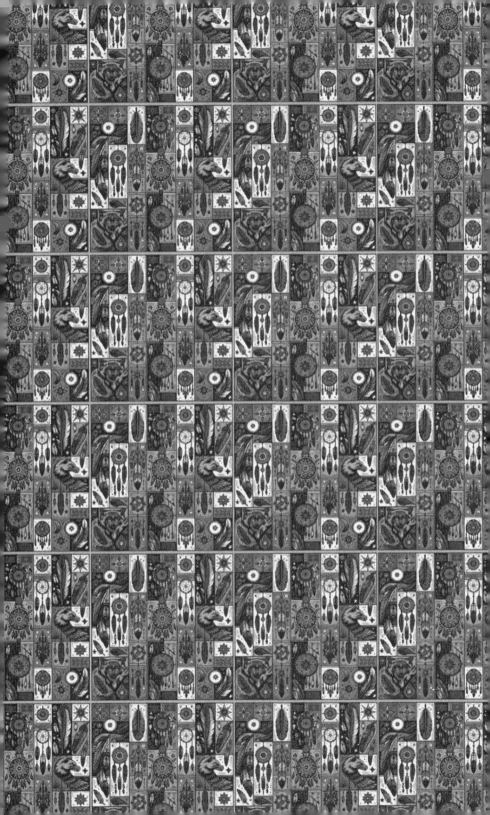

TABLE OF CONTENTS
A

$$\Omega$$

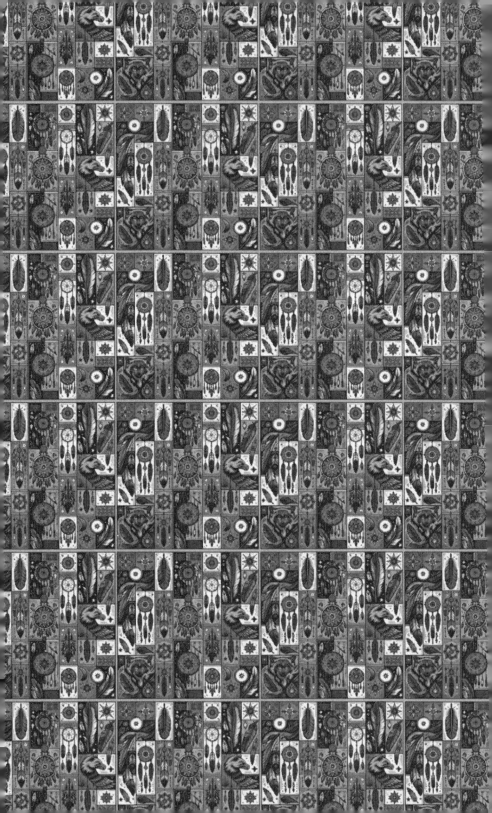

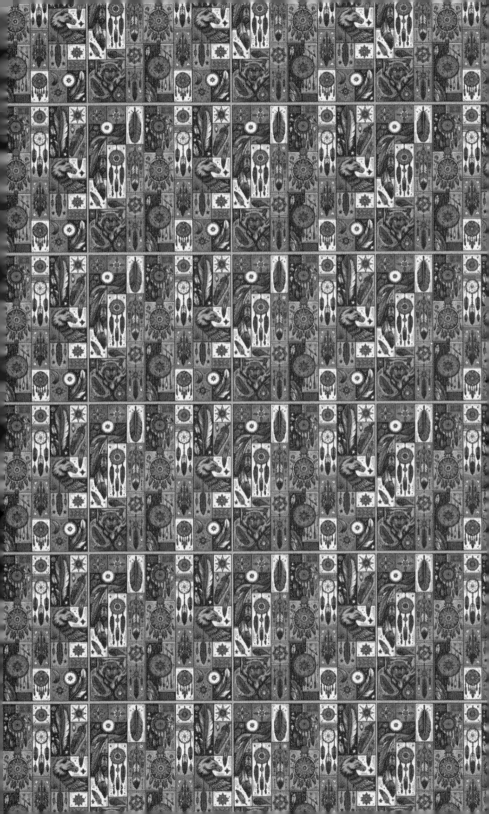

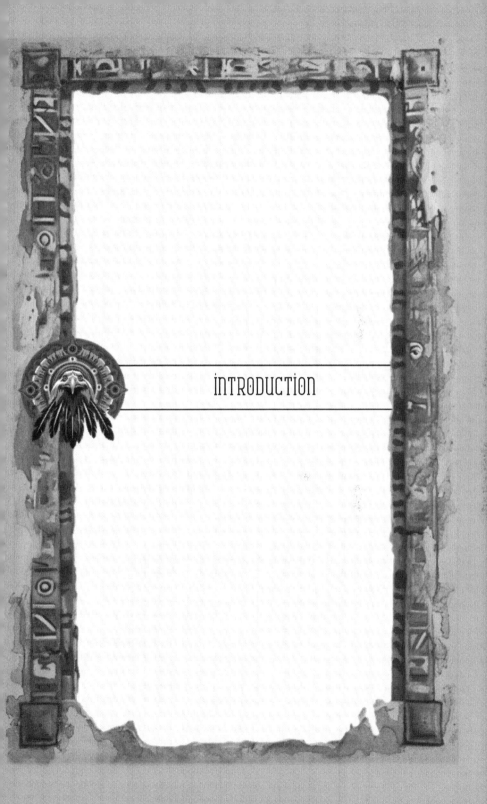

INTRODUCTION

In the atlas of humanity's existence, indigenous spiritualities stand as complex themes charted over millennia, connecting people to the land, the cosmos, and the profound mysteries of life. Across the giant expanse of North America, starting from the frigid Arctic to the sun-drenched deserts, and from the verdant forests to the windswept plains, indigenous peoples have nurtured a myriad of complex belief systems, rituals, and cosmologies. These spiritual traditions, deeply founded in the landscapes that sustain them, reflect a profound reverence for the natural world, the cycles of life, and the lasting connection between past, present, and future. This adventure begins on a adventure through the diverse and profound spiritual traditions of indigenous peoples in North America. It is a adventure of discovery, one that traverses the contours of history, culture, and belief systems, seeking to understand the profound wisdom embedded in the spiritual atlases of these ancient cultures. From the ancestral Puebloan cosmology of the Southwest to the Inuit spirituality of the Arctic, starting from the Lakota sweat lodge ceremonies to the Haudenosaunee Great Law of Peace, this adventure will dive into the opulent and multifaceted worlds of indigenous spiritualities that have endured, adapted, and thrived throughout centuries of change and challenge.

At the heart of these indigenous spiritualities lies a deep and abiding connection to the land. The physical territory is imbued with spiritual significance, with rivers, mountains, animals, and plants serving as not just resources but as living entities with their own consciousness and power. This spiritual connection manifests in complex rituals, dances, songs, and ceremonies that honor the land and its gifts. Whether it is the sacred mountain of the Navajo, the bear dance of the Ute, or the totem poles of the Northwest Coast, the natural world is celebrated as a source of spiritual encouragement and guidance. These spiritual traditions also offer profound insights into the relationship between humans and the spiritual world. Shamans adventure to otherworldly worlds to seek guidance and healing. Vision quests offer individuals a transformative experience of self-discovery and connection to the divine. The complexities of animal totemism decode the deep kinship between humans and the animal kingdom, bridging the gap between the physical and the spiritual.

Moreso, indigenous spiritualities reflect the resilience and adaptability of these cultures in the face of colonization, displacement, and cultural suppression. Despite centuries of adversity, these traditions have persisted, evolving and blending with other belief systems while maintaining their core values and worldviews. The Ghost Dance, for example, emerged as a pan-Indian movement in response to colonization, offering a vision of cultural revitalization and unity. Similarly, the Nez Perce

Longhouse religion stands for a unique fusion of Christian and traditional beliefs, demonstrating the adaptability of indigenous spirituality. And as we begin on this adventure, it is essential to approach these indigenous spiritualities with respect, humility, and a recognition of their lasting significance. These traditions are not relics of the past but living, breathing expressions of the human spirit in constant dialogue with the natural and supernatural worlds. They offer profound insights into the enmeshment of all life, the importance of community, and the lasting wisdom that vibes through the ages.

Throughout this adventure, we will dive into the complexities of each indigenous spirituality, seeking to understand their historical origins, core beliefs, rituals, and contemporary significance. From the Lakota sweat lodge ceremonies that cleanse the body and spirit to the Ancestral Puebloan cosmology that charts complex stories of creation and existence, each tradition offers a unique perspective on the human adventure through this world and the next. The indigenous spiritualities of North America are a confirmation of the lasting power of the human spirit to connect with the divine, the natural world, and the collective wisdom of ancestors. They invite us to step beyond the bounds of our own cultural lenses and into a world where the land is sacred, animals are kin, and the past, present, and future are intertwined. Through this adventure, we begin on a adventure of understanding and appreciation for the opulent atlas of indigenous spiritualities that continue to shape the lives and worldviews of indigenous peoples across North America.

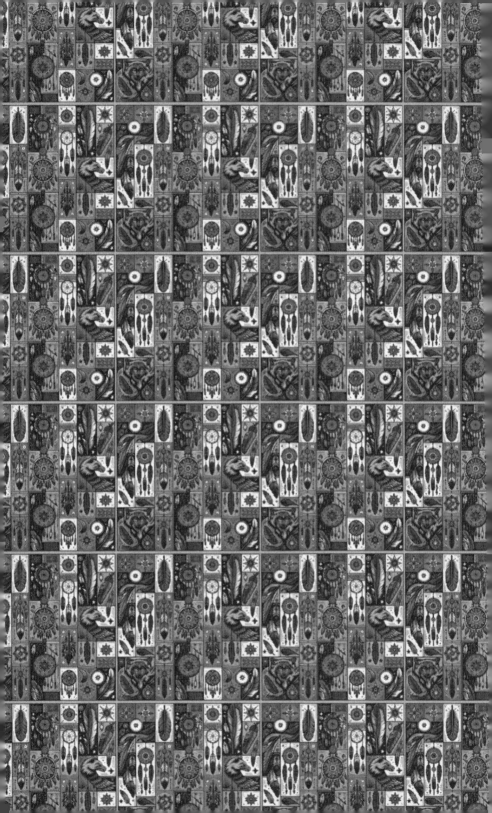

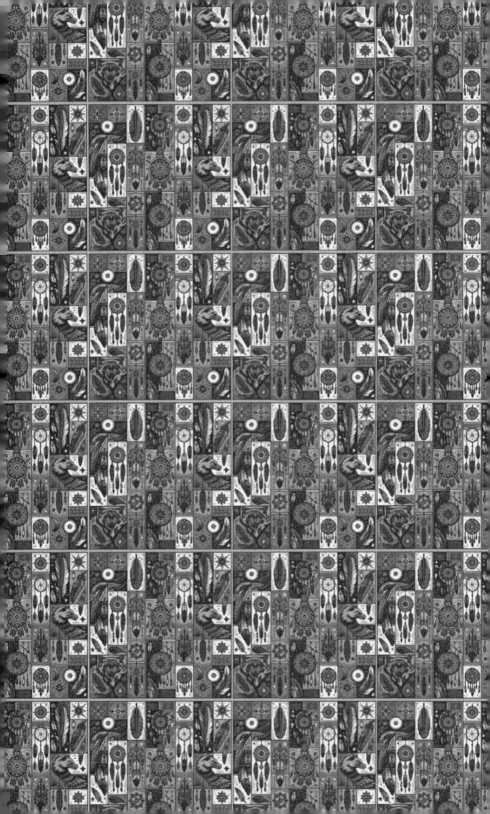

I: WAKAN TANKA

The concept of Wakan Tanka, often translated as "Great Mystery" or "Great Spirit," is a central and profound aspect of the Lakota Sioux's spiritual and religious beliefs. To understand Wakan Tanka, one must dive deep into the heart of Lakota cosmology, which is intricately intertwined with their history, culture, and worldview. This spiritual entity stands for far more than a mere deity; it includes the essence of the Lakota understanding of the universe, the interconnection of all things, and the path to spiritual enlightenment. The Lakota people are indigenous to the Great Plains of North America, specifically the region now known as South Dakota, North Dakota, Nebraska, Wyoming, and Montana. Their traditional way of life was deeply connected to the natural world, as they were nomadic hunters and gatherers who depended on buffalo for sustenance and materials. This intimate relationship with the land and its resources profoundly shaped their spiritual beliefs, including their understanding of Wakan Tanka.

Wakan Tanka is not a conventional god in the Western sense. It is a spiritual force that permeates the entire cosmos, transcending human comprehension. The word "Wakan" itself is a term that conveys the idea of sacredness, holiness, and mystery, while "Tanka" means "great" or "large." Therefore, Wakan Tanka is often described as the "Great Mystery" or the "Great Spirit" because it stands for the profound, awe-inspiring, and unknowable nature of the divine. At the core of the Lakota belief system is the idea that everything in the universe is interconnected and imbued with the presence of Wakan Tanka. This includes not just living beings but also elements of the natural world, like animals, plants, rocks, and even the wind and the stars. In the Lakota view, there is no strict separation between the physical and the spiritual worlds; they are intertwined and interdependent.

The Lakota people believe that Wakan Tanka communicates with them through visions, dreams, and personal experiences. These spiritual encounters are often facilitated through rituals and ceremonies conducted by tribal shamans or spiritual leaders. The sweat lodge ceremony, vision quests, and the Sun Dance are among the practices that serve as conduits for connecting with Wakan Tanka. These ceremonies are deeply symbolic and involve fasting, prayer, and various physical ordeals meant to purify the body and open the mind to divine guidance. One of the most fundamental aspects of the Lakota worldview is the concept of the "Four Directions" or the "Four Winds." These cardinal directions—north, south, east, and west—are believed to be associated with specific spiritual powers and aspects of Wakan Tanka. The Lakota ceremonial circle, often marked by stones or other natural materials, stands for the harmonious relationship of these forces. This circle is not just a physical space for rituals but also a symbolic representation of the cosmos and the enmeshment of all things within it.

Each of the Four Directions has its own significance. The East is associated with new beginnings, enlightenment, and the rising sun. The South stands for growth, abundance, and the warmth of summer. The West symbolizes introspection, reflection, and the setting sun. The North is connected to wisdom, challenges, and the cold of winter. Together, these directions form a holistic understanding of existence, embodying the cyclical nature of life, death, and rebirth.

In the Lakota cosmology, Wakan Tanka is not distant or removed from human affairs but is deeply involved in the daily lives of the people. The Lakota seek to maintain a harmonious relationship with Wakan Tanka by living in accordance with the natural order and following ethical principles. Respect for all living beings, gratitude for the gifts of the Earth, and humility in the face of the Great Mystery are essential virtues in the Lakota way of life. Rituals and ceremonies are essential means of expressing this reverence for Wakan Tanka and maintaining spiritual balance. The Sun Dance, for example, is a powerful ritual in which participants pierce their flesh as a symbolic sacrifice, connecting themselves with the suffering of the buffalo and the Earth. This act of selflessness and endurance is seen as a way to gain spiritual insight and healing.

The concept of Wakan Tanka also plays a necessary place in the Lakota understanding of healing and medicine. Traditional healers, known as medicine men or women, believe that illness is often caused by spiritual imbalances or disharmony with the natural world. They work to restore these harmonies through rituals, herbs, and spiritual practices, seeking guidance from Wakan Tanka to facilitate the healing process.

It is important to note that the Lakota belief system is not monolithic, as there are regional variations and individual interpretations of Wakan Tanka within the Lakota Nation. Additionally, the arrival of European settlers and the forced assimilation of indigenous peoples led to significant disruptions in Lakota spirituality. Despite these challenges, many Lakota people continue to preserve and revitalize their traditional beliefs and practices, including their deep connection to Wakan Tanka. The concept of Wakan Tanka, the Great Mystery, lies at the heart of Lakota spirituality and worldview. It stands for a profound, interconnected, and ever-present force that infuses all aspects of the Lakota way of life. Wakan Tanka is not a distant deity but a living presence in the natural world and within the hearts of the Lakota people. It acts as a source of guidance, encouragement, and healing, connecting individuals to the giant and mysterious cosmos while reminding them of their responsibilities to maintain harmony with all living beings. The

Lakota's deep respect for the Great Mystery continues to be a source of wisdom and encouragement for seekers of truth and spiritual understanding worldwide, transcending time and place.

II: HEYOKA

At the heart of Heyoka rituals lies the sacred clown, an individual who defies convention by speaking, moving, and reacting in an opposite or contrarian fashion to the norms of society. These ceremonies offer profound insights into the complexities of Lakota belief systems, where the disruption of established patterns acts as a means of spiritual awakening and transformation. In Lakota culture, the Heyoka is regarded as a spiritual teacher and a conduit to the divine. The term "Heyoka" can be translated as "sacred clown" or "contrary," but its meaning goes far beyond these simplistic labels. Heyokas possess a unique place within the tribe, often marked by their unconventional behavior and the ability to perceive the world from a different perspective. Their actions are seen as a reflection of the sacred and mysterious nature of Wakan Tanka, the Great Mystery.

The concept of Heyoka is deeply founded in the Lakota worldview, which places great importance on balance and harmony in all aspects of life. Heyokas, by their very nature, disrupt the ordinary flow of existence, challenging the status quo and forcing individuals to confront their assumptions and biases. Through their actions, Heyokas highlight the absurdities of humanity's behavior and the bounds of conventional thinking. Heyoka ceremonies typically involve a series of rituals and performances that show the contrarian behavior of the sacred clowns. These ceremonies are often held within the context of larger tribal gatherings or seasonal events. While the specific details of Heyoka ceremonies can vary among different Lakota groups and communities, there are common elements that provide insight into their spiritual significance. One of the most distinctive features of Heyoka ceremonies is the use of humor and satire. Heyokas employ laughter and absurdity to provoke self-reflection and challenge social norms. Through their antics, they expose the contradictions and hypocrisies of everyday life. This form of humor is not meant to belittle or demean but rather to create a space for introspection and transformation. During Heyoka ceremonies, participants may witness the sacred clowns engaging in actions that defy logic and expectation. They may walk backward, speak in riddles, wear clothing inside out, or perform other actions that subvert ordinary behavior. These contrarian acts are not arbitrary but are deeply symbolic, representing a reversal of conventional thinking and a breaking of established patterns. The place of the Heyoka extends beyond mere entertainment; they are respected as spiritual catalysts. By disrupting the ordinary and challenging the comfortable, Heyokas push individuals to see the world in new ways. In doing so, they help people break free from the constraints of routine thinking and open themselves to the mysteries of the universe.

The Heyoka's contrarian behavior is not seen as random but as a manifestation of their connection to the spirit world. They are believed to possess a unique sensitivity to the unseen forces that shape human existence. Heyokas often receive visions and guidance from the spirit world, which they use to guide their actions during ceremonies. This connection to the spirit world underscores their place as spiritual intermediaries. In addition to their contrarian behavior, Heyokas are known for their use of sacred objects and tools in their ceremonies. These may include masks, rattles, and other items imbued with spiritual significance. Masks, in particular, are essential to Heyoka rituals, as they allow the sacred clowns to transform themselves into powerful and otherworldly beings. The act of donning a mask is a symbolic gesture that signifies the Heyoka's entry into the world of the sacred.

Heyoka ceremonies often involve dances and songs that are unique to these rituals. These dances are marked by their lively and unpredictable movements, mirroring the Heyoka's contrarian nature. The songs sung during these ceremonies carry deep spiritual meaning and are believed to invoke the presence of the divine. Drumming and chanting are integral to these performances, creating a rhythmic and trance-inducing atmosphere. While Heyoka ceremonies may appear chaotic and disordered to outsiders, they are, in fact, highly structured and purposeful. Each action, gesture, and word has meaning within the context of the ritual. The disruption caused by the Heyokas is intentional, designed to shake people out of their complacency and challenge their preconceived notions.

One of the central themes of Heyoka ceremonies is the idea of "sacred chaos." This concept acknowledges that the universe is inherently unpredictable and that order can emerge from disorder. Heyokas embody this principle by introducing chaos and uncertainty into the ritual space, forcing participants to confront the unpredictable nature of existence. Through this process, individuals may experience moments of profound insight and spiritual awakening. Another key aspect of Heyoka ceremonies is their ability to bring healing and balance to the community. The disruption caused by the Heyokas acts as a release valve for pent-up tensions and grievances within the tribe. By highlighting the absurdities of humanity's behavior and providing a platform for humor and satire, Heyokas help to diffuse conflicts and promote social cohesion.

Heyoka ceremonies are not limited to a single event but are part of a larger spiritual adventure. Individuals may undergo a transformation through their interactions with Heyokas, leading to a deeper understanding of themselves and the world around them. It is believed that the Heyoka's ability to disrupt established patterns can lead to personal growth and enlightenment. Heyoka ceremonies are a unique and profound aspect of Lakota spirituality, founded in the belief that disruption and contrarian behavior can lead to spiritual awakening and transformation. The sacred clowns who lead these rituals challenge social norms, provoke self-reflection, and serve as conduits to the spirit world. Through humor, satire, and sacred chaos, Heyokas create a space for individuals to break free from routine thinking and open themselves to the mysteries of the universe. These ceremonies are a confirmation of the deep spiritual wisdom of the Lakota people and their profound understanding of the enmeshment of all things.

III: Inipi

Now about Inipi, which translates to "to live again" in the Lakota language. The Inipi, commonly referred to as the sweat lodge ceremony, holds profound significance within Lakota spirituality. It acts as a transformative ritual designed to cleanse the body, mind, and spirit, facilitating a deep connection with the divine and the natural world. To comprehend the essence of the Inipi is to adventure into the heart of Lakota cosmology and their lasting reverence for the sacredness of all life. The Inipi is an ancient and sacred ceremony deeply founded in Lakota tradition. It stands for a necessary element of their spiritual practice, serving both as a rite of passage and a means of seeking guidance and healing from Wakan Tanka, the Great Mystery. Central to the ceremony is the sweat lodge, a small, domed structure constructed from willow branches and covered with blankets or hides. The sweat lodge symbolizes the womb of Mother Earth and is seen as a sacred space where participants can undergo a process of purification and rebirth.

The Inipi ceremony is typically conducted by a knowledgeable and experienced leader, often referred to as a "lodge keeper" or "sweat lodge leader." This individual plays a necessary place in guiding participants through the various stages of the ritual and invoking the presence of the divine. The ceremony typically begins with the lighting of a fire outside the sweat lodge, which heats volcanic stones, known as "grandfathers" or "stone people." These stones, when heated to a high temperature, serve as the central element for generating the intense heat and steam within the lodge.

The Inipi ceremony consists of several distinct phases, each imbued with profound spiritual meaning. Participants gather outside the sweat lodge and engage in prayers and songs to prepare themselves for the ritual. These prayers are meant to invoke the presence of the sacred and establish a connection with the spiritual world. The lodge keeper, as a spiritual guide, leads these initial prayers and sets the tone for the ceremony. Once the preliminary prayers and songs are completed, the participants enter the sweat lodge, typically in a clockwise direction, a movement that aligns with the natural flow of life in Lakota cosmology. The interior of the sweat lodge is intentionally dark and confined, symbolizing the womb of Mother Earth. The entrance of participants into this sacred space stands for a form of rebirth, where individuals shed their worldly concerns and enter into a state of vulnerability and receptivity. Inside the sweat lodge, participants sit in a circle around the central pit where the heated stones are placed. The lodge keeper, who acts as a spiritual intermediary, begins to pour water infused with herbs onto the red-hot stones. As the water contacts the stones, it transforms into steam, filling the sweat lodge with intense heat and moisture. This steam, often referred to as "the breath of Wakan Tanka," is believed to carry the spiritual essence and healing power of the sacred.

The combination of heat, steam, and the enclosed space of the sweat lodge induces a state of physical and spiritual purification. Participants sweat profusely, releasing toxins from their bodies and cleansing themselves of impurities. This physical purification is seen as a metaphor for the cleansing of the mind and spirit, allowing participants to let go of negative thoughts, emotions, and burdens they may carry.

Throughout the Inipi ceremony, prayers, songs, and chants are offered by the lodge keeper and participants. These sacred words and melodies are intended to invoke the presence of Wakan Tanka and the spirit of the natural world. Participants may also share their intentions, concerns, or desires during the ceremony, seeking guidance, healing, or spiritual insight. The Inipi is not solely a physical endurance test but a profound spiritual adventure. The heat and darkness of the sweat lodge serve as a metaphorical and experiential adventure deep into one's soul. Participants confront their fears, doubts, and vulnerabilities, seeking clarity and spiritual transformation. It is believed that the intense conditions of the sweat lodge facilitate a direct connection with the divine, enabling participants to receive guidance, visions, or insights from the spirit world.

The Inipi ceremony typically consists of multiple rounds, with the lodge keeper periodically adding additional water and heated stones to maintain the intensity of the experience. Each round may have a specific focus or theme, like healing, gratitude, or spiritual guidance. The lodge keeper may also offer teachings and stories that relate to the overall purpose of the ceremony.

One of the key teachings of the Inipi is the concept of enmeshment. Lakota spirituality focuses on the profound enmeshment of all living beings and the natural world. The sweat lodge ceremony reinforces this belief by creating a shared experience of purification and transformation. Participants recognize that they are not separate from the Earth or from one another but are part of a larger, interconnected nexus of existence. The Inipi ceremony concludes with a final round of prayers and songs, marking the culmination of the spiritual adventure within the sweat lodge. Participants exit the lodge, often in a counterclockwise direction, symbolizing their return to the outside world with a newfound sense of clarity, strength, and spiritual insight. Following the ceremony, it is customary for participants to engage in a period of reflection and sharing. This post-ceremony time allows individuals to process their experiences, discuss any visions or insights they received, and express their gratitude for the purification and guidance they received from Wakan Tanka and the spirit world.

The effects of the Inipi ceremony are far-reaching and deeply transformative. Participants often report a sense of renewal, emotional release, and a heightened connection to the natural world. The ceremony can also serve as a source of healing for individuals dealing with physical, emotional, or spiritual challenges.

In conclusion, the Inipi, or sweat lodge ceremony, is a profound and sacred rite within Lakota spirituality, designed to facilitate physical, emotional, and spiritual purification and transformation. Through the intense heat and steam of the sweat lodge, participants undergo a adventure of rebirth and renewal, shedding impurities and gaining insights from the spirit world. The Inipi embodies the enmeshment of all life and acts as a powerful means of seeking guidance, healing, and spiritual growth. It is a confirmation of the deep wisdom of the Lakota people and their lasting reverence for the sacredness of existence.

IV: Kachina Doll Magic

Certainly, noble seeker of truth, I shall now illuminate the mystical world of Kachina Doll Magic, a sacred and complex aspect of Hopi spiritual belief. The Hopi people, indigenous to the American Southwest, hold a profound reverence for the Kachinas, divine spirit beings that personify various aspects of the natural world and the cosmos. These sacred beings are not just revered but also represented in exquisitely crafted Kachina dolls, which serve as both artistic treasures and spiritual conduits.

At the heart of Hopi culture and spirituality lies the belief in the Kachinas, celestial intermediaries who mediate between the Hopi people and the supernatural world. The term "Kachina" is often used to refer to both the spirit beings themselves and the ceremonial dancers who impersonate them during religious rituals. These spirit beings are associated with the forces of nature, like rain, sun, clouds, plants, animals, and celestial bodies, and are believed to hold a necessary place in the balance and wellness of the Hopi community. Kachina ceremonies are a central component of Hopi religious life and are typically held during the winter months, known as the Kachina season. These ceremonies involve masked dancers, or Kachina dancers, who embody the spirit of the specific Kachina being represented. The purpose of these ceremonies is to bring rain, fertility, and spiritual blessings to the Hopi people and their land. Each

Kachina has its own unique attributes and symbolism, reflecting its place in the natural and spiritual world.

One of the most remarkable aspects of Hopi culture is the artistry and craftsmanship associated with Kachina dolls. Kachina dolls are carefully handcrafted by skilled Hopi artisans, often using traditional techniques passed down through generations. These dolls are more than mere toys or decorative items; they are sacred representations of the Kachina spirits and are respected as spiritual tools.

Kachina dolls are typically carved from cottonwood root, a material chosen for its lightness and ease of carving. The dolls are then adorned with elaborate paintwork, feathers, clothing, and other materials to accurately depict the specific Kachina being represented. The level of detail and craftsmanship in Kachina dolls is truly awe-inspiring, with each doll serving as a miniature work of art that captures the essence of the corresponding Kachina spirit.The creation of Kachina dolls is a highly specialized craft within the Hopi community, and doll makers are regarded with great respect and admiration. The process of making these dolls is a sacred undertaking, and artisans often engage in prayer and meditation to ensure that the dolls are imbued with the spiritual essence of the Kachina they represent.

The purpose of Kachina dolls goes beyond their aesthetic appeal. These dolls serve a necessary place in Hopi religious and cultural life. They are used to educate the younger generation about the Kachina spirits, their attributes, and their significance in Hopi cosmology. Kachina dolls are often given to Hopi children as tools for learning and spiritual connection. Through these dolls, children gain an understanding of the Kachina beings and their place in the cycle of life and the natural world. Kachina dolls also hold a central place in the Kachina ceremonies themselves. During the ceremonies, the Kachina dancers present dolls to members of the community, including children. These dolls are not mere gifts but are believed to carry the blessings and spiritual power of the Kachina beings they represent. Receiving a Kachina doll during a ceremony is seen as a form of spiritual initiation, symbolizing a connection between the recipient and the Kachina spirit. Kachina dolls also serve as a form of communication with the spirit world. Hopi individuals may use these dolls in personal rituals and prayers to seek the guidance, protection, or blessings of specific Kachina beings. The dolls are believed to serve as intermediaries between the earthly world and the supernatural, carrying messages and intentions to the Kachina spirits. It is important to note that Kachina dolls are not respected as idols or objects of worship in the same way that deities are revered in some other religious traditions. Instead, they are regarded as representations and embodiments of the Kachina spirits, serving as tangible reminders of the sacred forces that influence the Hopi way of life. In addition to their place in religious and spiritual contexts, Kachina dolls have garnered international acclaim as works of art. Collectors and enthusiasts from around the world recognize the beauty and cultural significance of these dolls. The complex craftsmanship and attention to detail in Kachina dolls have led to their inclusion in museum collections and art galleries, where they are celebrated for their aesthetic and cultural value.

In conclusion, Kachina Doll Magic is a sacred and profound aspect of Hopi spiritual belief and cultural heritage. The Kachina dolls, carefully crafted representations of the Kachina spirits, serve as both educational tools and spiritual conduits within the Hopi community. These dolls embody the enmeshment of the Hopi people with the natural world and the spiritual world, offering blessings, guidance, and a deep appreciation for the sacred forces that shape their lives. Kachina Doll Magic is a confirmation of the artistry, spirituality, and lasting cultural richness of the Hopi people.

V: GHOST DANCE

Certainly, noble seeker of truth, I shall now dive into the historical and spiritual phenomenon known as the Ghost Dance, a pan-Indian movement that emerged in the late 19th century. Founded in indigenous spirituality and prophesying a rebirth of Native American cultures, the Ghost Dance holds a significant place in the history of Native American resistance and revival during a tumultuous period of American history.

The Ghost Dance movement originated in the context of immense hardship and suffering faced by Native American tribes in the late 19th century. Decades of westward expansion, forced removals, and broken treaties had left indigenous communities dispossessed, demoralized, and devastated by disease and starvation. In this climate of despair, a new spiritual movement emerged as a response to the dire circumstances facing Native American peoples. The central figure associated with the Ghost Dance movement was a Paiute prophet named Wovoka, also known as Jack Wilson. In 1889, Wovoka experienced a series of visions during a solar eclipse, during which he claimed to have received a message from the spirit world. According to Wovoka's teachings, the spirits conveyed a message of hope and transformation to Native American communities. He prophesied that if indigenous people embraced the Ghost Dance, participated in its rituals, and lived in peace, the spirits would intervene, leading to a rebirth of Native American cultures and a return of the ancestral lands.

The core belief of the Ghost Dance was the imminent arrival of an "Indian Messiah" or a "Messiah of the Native American people" who would help restore indigenous sovereignty, heal the sick, and bring about an era of peace and abundance. Wovoka himself was seen as a messenger of this prophetic vision, rather than the Messiah. The message of the Ghost Dance held immense appeal for Native American communities who yearned for an end to their suffering and a revival of their traditional ways of life. The Ghost Dance ceremony itself was a spiritual and communal gathering marked by dance, singing, and ritual. Participants would form a circle and move in a counterclockwise direction, symbolizing a return to the old ways. The dance was accompanied by songs and chants that conveyed the messages and visions received by Wovoka. Central to the ceremony was the wearing of special Ghost Dance shirts, believed to hold protective and healing powers. These shirts were adorned with symbols and designs that were thought to connect the wearer to the spiritual world.

The Ghost Dance spread rapidly among Native American tribes across the Western United States, starting from the Great Basin to the Plains. It resonated deeply with indigenous communities that searched out a path to cultural revival and the restoration of their traditional practices. The movement transcended tribal bounds, uniting diverse Native American groups in a shared sense of hope and purpose. The growing popularity of the Ghost Dance movement, however, raised concerns among U.S. government officials and settlers. The movement was often misinterpreted as a militant or messianic uprising, and authorities feared that it could lead to further unrest among Native American populations. As a result, government agents and military personnel closely monitored Ghost Dance ceremonies and searched out to suppress the movement.

One of the most tragic and infamous events associated with the Ghost Dance movement occurred at Wounded Knee, South Dakota, in December 1890. Tensions had been escalating between the U.S. Army and the Lakota Sioux, who were practicing the Ghost Dance as a form of resistance and cultural revitalization. On December 29, 1890, U.S. troops confronted a group of Lakota at Wounded Knee Creek, and a tragic confrontation ensued. In the end, hundreds of Lakota, including women and children, lost their lives in what became known as the Wounded Knee Massacre. The Wounded Knee Massacre marked a devastating and traumatic episode in the history of Native American-European relations. It also served as a turning point in the Ghost Dance movement. The violent suppression of the movement by government authorities led to a decline in its popularity among some tribes, as many came to associate the Ghost Dance with tragedy and loss. Despite the tragic events at Wounded Knee, the Ghost Dance movement continued to hold significance for some Native American communities, and its spiritual teachings endured. The movement's emphasis on unity, cultural revival, and the hope for a better future continued to vibe with indigenous peoples throughout the 20th century and beyond.

In conclusion, the Ghost Dance was a pan-Indian spiritual movement that emerged in the late 19th century as a response to the dire circumstances facing Native American tribes. Founded in indigenous spirituality and prophesying a rebirth of Native American cultures, the Ghost Dance offered hope and a sense of purpose during a period of profound adversity. While the movement faced tragic suppression and misunderstanding, its lasting heritage lies in its place as a symbol of resilience and cultural revival within Native American communities, reflecting the deep yearning for healing and restoration in the face of immense challenges.

VI: SUN DANCE

Certainly, noble seeker of truth, I shall now illuminate the profound and sacred ceremony known as the Sun Dance, practiced by numerous Native American tribes, particularly on the Great Plains. The Sun Dance is a deeply spiritual and transformative ritual that involves fasting, prayer, and personal sacrifice, serving as a central element of indigenous belief systems and cultural expression. The Sun Dance holds a revered place in the spiritual and cultural traditions of many Native American tribes, including the Lakota, Cheyenne, Arapaho, and many others of the Great Plains region. It is a complex and multifaceted ceremony that is performed during the summer months, typically around the time of the summer solstice, when the sun is at its zenith.

At the heart of the Sun Dance is the concept of renewal, sacrifice, and the interconnection between all living beings and the natural world. The ceremony is a means of seeking spiritual guidance, healing, and communal solidarity while also honoring the sun, which is regarded as a source of life and power. One of the central features of the Sun Dance is the construction of a sacred arbor, or dance lodge, which acts as the ceremonial space for the ritual. The arbor is typically a large, circular structure made of wooden poles and covered with branches or hides. It is carefully prepared and symbolically stands for the universe and the sacred circle of life.

The Sun Dance is led by a spiritual leader, often referred to as a "Sun Dance chief" or "medicine man." This individual plays a necessary place in guiding the ceremony and ensuring its proper execution. Participants in the Sun Dance are known as "dancers," and they come from various tribes and communities to take part in the ritual.

The preparation for the Sun Dance is rigorous and demanding. Dancers undergo a period of purification, which may include fasting, sweat lodge ceremonies, and other forms of spiritual preparation. During the days leading up to the ceremony, dancers abstain from food and water, symbolizing their sacrifice and commitment to the ritual. The central element of the Sun Dance involves the dancers piercing their chest or back with wooden skewers or bone awls. These objects are then attached to a ceremonial pole in the center of the arbor, and the dancers dance around the pole, pulling against the skewers as an act of personal sacrifice and endurance. This physical and spiritual ordeal is seen as a means of offering oneself to the Creator and seeking blessings for the community. Throughout the Sun Dance, participants engage in prayer, song, and dance, with the beat of a drum providing a rhythmic and ceremonial backdrop. The songs and chants are deeply spiritual, conveying messages of gratitude, healing, and communal unity. The dance itself is a powerful and symbolic act of renewal and rebirth.

The Sun Dance is not solely an individual experience but a communal one, reflecting the enmeshment of all living beings. It acts as a means of seeking blessings and guidance not just for the dancers but also for their families, communities, and the natural world. The ritual underscores the belief that personal sacrifice can bring about collective healing and renewal. The culmination of the Sun Dance often involves a symbolic rebirth for the dancers. After completing their dance and sacrifice, the skewers are removed from their flesh, and they emerge from the ordeal transformed and spiritually renewed. This act of emerging from the ceremonial pole is seen as a metaphorical rebirth, signifying the restoration of balance and harmony in the world.

The Sun Dance also includes other elements, like the making of prayer ties, the offering of gifts, and the sharing of communal meals. These activities reinforce the sense of community and enmeshment that underlie the ceremony. The giving of gifts and the sharing of food serve as acts of reciprocity and gratitude toward the Creator and the spirits.

The Sun Dance is a sacred and highly respected ceremony, and the knowledge and practices associated with it are passed down through generations within indigenous communities. In the past, the Sun Dance faced suppression and persecution by colonial authorities, but it has endured and continues to be practiced as a means of preserving cultural traditions and connecting with the spiritual world.

The Sun Dance is a profoundly spiritual and transformative ceremony practiced by numerous Native American tribes, particularly on the Great Plains. It involves fasting, prayer, and personal sacrifice, serving as a means of seeking spiritual guidance, healing, and renewal. The ritual underscores the enmeshment of all living beings and the natural world, and it reflects the lasting cultural and spiritual richness of indigenous traditions in North America.

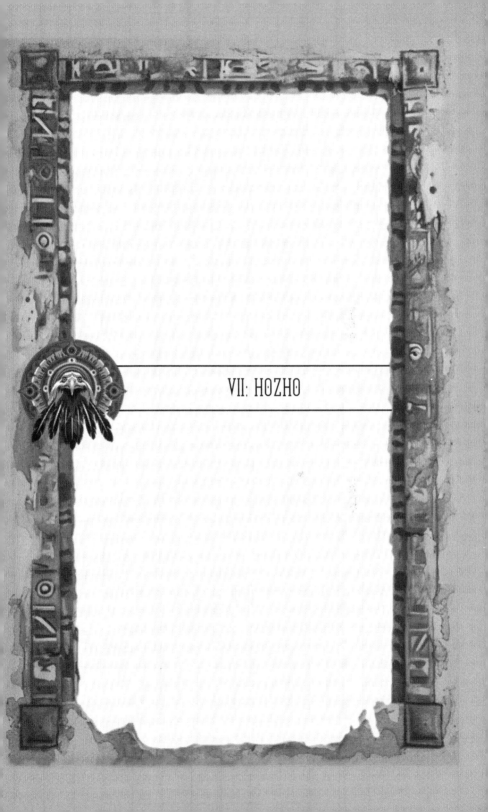

VII: HOZHO

Certainly, noble seeker of truth, I shall now illuminate the profound and foundational concept of Hozho, a central tenet in Navajo spirituality. Founded in the Navajo language, Hozho can be translated as "harmony," but its significance goes far beyond a mere word. It includes a profound worldview that centers on balance, beauty, harmony, and wellness, reflecting the enmeshment of all aspects of life within the Navajo cultural and spiritual scaffolding. Hozho is at the heart of Navajo cosmology and is charted into the map of daily life and ceremonial practices. It is not merely an abstract concept but a guiding principle that informs Navajo values, actions, and relationships with the natural and spiritual worlds.

At its core, Hozho embodies the idea that all things in the universe are interconnected and interdependent. It recognizes that the natural world, human beings, and the spiritual world are intricately linked, and that maintaining harmony and balance is essential for the wellness of individuals and the community as a whole. One of the key aspects of Hozho is the belief that beauty and balance are not superficial or arbitrary but fundamental to the order of the universe. The Navajo people believe that the Creator, or Diyin Dine'e, created the world in a state of Hozho, and it is the responsibility of humans to uphold and restore this state of harmony.

In Navajo philosophy, beauty is not limited to aesthetics but extends to the way individuals conduct themselves in the world. Living in accordance with Hozho means acting with integrity, compassion, and respect for all beings. It involves treating others with kindness and upholding ethical principles.

The pursuit of Hozho also involves maintaining physical, mental, and spiritual wellness. Navajo ceremonies and rituals, like the Blessingway ceremony (Hózhǫǫjí), are performed to restore balance and harmony to individuals who may have strayed from the path of Hozho. These ceremonies involve prayers, songs, and rituals aimed at aligning the individual with the natural and spiritual forces that govern the universe.

The concept of Hozho extends to the relationship between humans and the natural world. Navajo people have a deep reverence for the land, animals, plants, and elements, recognizing their place in the complex nexus of life. Practices like sustainable land stewardship, herbal medicine, and animal husbandry are guided by the principles of Hozho, ensuring a harmonious relationship with the environment. In Navajo art and craftsmanship, Hozho is mirrored in the complex designs, patterns, and symbolism found in rugs, jewelry, pottery, and other traditional forms of expression. These artistic creations are not just beautiful but are imbued with spiritual significance and serve as a means of conveying stories, prayers, and blessings. The concept of Hozho also plays a necessary place in Navajo storytelling and oral traditions. Stories and myths are passed down through generations to impart wisdom and convey the importance of living in harmony with the natural and spiritual worlds. These narratives reinforce the idea that maintaining Hozho is a lifelong adventure and a collective responsibility.

In closing, Hozho is a foundational and profound concept in Navajo spirituality, emphasizing balance, beauty, harmony, and wellness in all aspects of life. It reflects the enmeshment of the natural, human, and spiritual worlds and guides Navajo values, ethics, and cultural practices. Hozho is not merely a philosophical ideal but a way of life that honors the Creator, the land, and all living beings, embodying the lasting wisdom and cultural richness of the Navajo people.

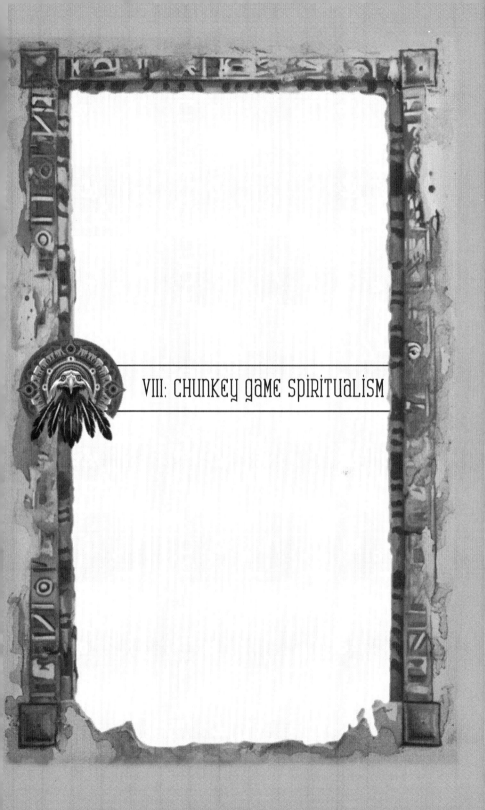

VIII: CHUNKEY GAME SPIRITUALISM

Certainly, noble seeker of truth, I shall now adventure through the interesting world of Chunkey Game Spiritualism, an ancient game played by the Mississippian culture that is believed to have held deep religious and spiritual significance. This ancient indigenous game offers valuable insights into the complex relationship between recreation, spirituality, and social cohesion within Native American societies of the time. Chunkey, also spelled as "chunkey" or "chenco," was a game that held particular importance among the Mississippian culture, which thrived in the southeastern United States from approximately 800 CE to 1600 CE. The game involved a stone disc or "chunkey stone" and a spear-like stick, and it was typically played on specially prepared rectangular holding fields.

The chunkey stone, which was often cylindrical or disc-shaped, served as the central element of the game. These stones were carefully crafted from various types of stone, including steatite, and often featured complex designs and carvings. The stones were highly valued and regarded as sacred objects. The objective of the Chunkey game was for participants to roll the chunkey stone across the holding field, while others attempted to throw their spears or sticks in an attempt to land them as close as possible to the stone's final resting place. The player whose spear came closest to the stone's final position was declared the winner.

While the Chunkey game might, on the surface, appear as a form of sport or recreation, it held profound spiritual and religious significance for the Mississippian culture. The game was not merely an athletic competition but was intertwined with the belief systems and cosmology of the society.

Several aspects of the Chunkey game point to its spiritual importance:

Ritualistic Elements
Chunkey games were often accompanied by elaborate rituals and ceremonies. Before the game commenced, participants would engage in prayers and offerings to invoke the favor of the spirits. The ritualistic aspect of the game reinforced the idea that Chunkey was more than just entertainment; it was a form of communion with the spiritual world.

Sacred Stones
The chunkey stones themselves were regarded as sacred objects, often adorned with symbols and carvings that held spiritual significance. These stones were treated with reverence and respect, emphasizing their connection to the spiritual world.

Cosmic Symbolism
The rolling of the chunkey stone across the holding field was seen as a representation of celestial

movements, particularly the path of the sun across the sky. This cosmic symbolism linked the game to broader cosmological beliefs, underscoring its spiritual dimension.

Community and Social Cohesion

Chunkey games often brought together members of the community, encouraging social cohesion and unity. In indigenous societies, communal activities often had spiritual undertones, emphasizing the importance of collective harmony and wellness.

Divination and Prophecy

Some accounts suggest that Chunkey games were used for divination and prophecy. The outcomes of the games were interpreted as messages from the spirits, offering guidance or predictions about future events.

In addition to its spiritual and religious aspects, Chunkey also served as a means of diplomacy and conflict resolution among different Mississippian communities. Games could be used to establish alliances, resolve disputes, or celebrate important events. The decline of the Mississippian culture and the eventual disruption of their societies by European colonization led to the waning of Chunkey and many other indigenous traditions. However, efforts have been made to preserve and revive the game in modern times, both as a form of cultural revitalization and as a way to reconnect with ancestral spiritual practices.

Chunkey Game Spiritualism reflects the complex relationship between recreation, spirituality, and social cohesion within the Mississippian culture. While on the surface, Chunkey may appear as a simple game, it was deeply founded in indigenous belief systems and cosmology. The rituals, sacred objects, and cosmic symbolism associated with Chunkey underscore its profound spiritual significance and its place as a cultural and communal practice that searched out to maintain harmony with the spiritual world and among members of the community.

IX: ANCESTRAL PUEBLOAN PEOPLES

Certainly, noble seeker of truth, I shall now dive into the complex spiritual beliefs and cosmological views of the Ancestral Puebloan peoples, shedding light on the opulent atlas of their cosmology and the profound connection between their spirituality and the natural world.

The Ancestral Puebloan peoples, also known as the Anasazi, inhabited the southwestern region of North America, particularly the present-day Four Corners region, which includes parts of present-day Arizona, Colorado, New Mexico, and Utah. Their culture flourished from approximately 200 CE to 1300 CE. At the core of their way of life was a deep and complex cosmology that guided their understanding of the universe, their relationship with the land, and their spiritual practices.

Sacred Territory

Central to Ancestral Puebloan cosmology was the belief in the sacredness of the natural territory. The people believed that the land itself possessed spiritual power and was inhabited by ancestral spirits. Specific geographical features, like mesas, canyons, and springs, were respected as sacred sites, and they played a necessary place in religious ceremonies and rituals. These sites served as points of connection between the earthly world and the spirit world.

Kachinas

The Ancestral Puebloans held a belief in Kachinas, spirit beings that were seen as intermediaries between the human and spiritual worlds. Kachinas were believed to bring blessings, fertility, and guidance to the community. The Kachina religion involved elaborate ceremonies, dances, and masked impersonations of these spirit beings. Each Kachina had its own attributes and symbolism, reflecting different aspects of the natural world and spiritual forces.

Cycles of Time

Ancestral Puebloan cosmology was deeply attuned to the cyclical nature of time. They believed in the existence of multiple worlds or "world ages," each with its own set of events and challenges. These world ages were cyclical and were marked by cosmic events, like the movement of celestial bodies. The Ancestral Puebloans searched out to align themselves with the cosmic rhythms and navigate the transitions between world ages.

Petroglyphs and Pictographs

The Ancestral Puebloans left behind an opulent heritage of rock art in the form of petroglyphs (carvings) and pictographs (paintings) on rock surfaces. These artworks often described celestial bodies, animals, and spiritual beings. They served as a form of communication with the spirit world and as a means of recording their cosmological beliefs.

Kivas

Central to Ancestral Puebloan communities were kivas, subterranean ceremonial chambers. Kivas were not just places of worship but also represented the symbolic womb of Mother Earth. Ceremonial activities, including prayer, dance, and rituals, were conducted within kivas to maintain harmony and balance with the natural and spiritual worlds.

Agricultural Rituals

Agriculture played a necessary place in the lives of the Ancestral Puebloans, and their spiritual beliefs were closely tied to farming practices. Rituals and ceremonies were performed to ensure successful crops and to acknowledge the necessary place of rain and seasonal cycles in sustaining life.

Clan and Ancestral Connections

Ancestral Puebloan cosmology emphasized the importance of clan and ancestral connections. Ancestors were believed to continue to influence the lives of their descendants, and honoring and remembering them through rituals and ceremonies was essential to maintaining harmony within the community.

Reciprocity and Balance

A fundamental principle in Ancestral Puebloan cosmology was the concept of reciprocity and balance. The people believed in the need to give back to the natural world and the spirit beings in exchange for their blessings. This reciprocal relationship was seen as essential for the wellness of the community.

In conclusion, Ancestral Puebloan cosmology was a complex and deeply spiritual belief system that interwove the natural world, celestial forces, and the spirit world. Their cosmology guided their daily lives, rituals, and interactions with the land and each other. It mirrored a profound respect for the enmeshment of all things and the lasting heritage of their deep spiritual connection to the American Southwest's unique territory.

X: PEYOTE RELIGION

The Peyote Religion is a sacred and deeply spiritual tradition centered around the ceremonial use of the peyote cactus (scientifically known as Lophophora williamsii). This religious practice is particularly prominent within the Native American Church, a religious movement that emerged in the late 19th century among various indigenous tribes in North America. At its core, the Peyote Religion focuses on communion with the divine, seeking spiritual guidance, and encouraging a sense of unity among its practitioners.

The ceremonial use of peyote is founded in the belief that the cactus is a sacred and powerful conduit to the spiritual world. Peyote is consumed during religious ceremonies, often in the form of a tea or a chewable preparation, with participants ingesting it to induce altered states of consciousness. This altered state is believed to facilitate communication with the divine, connect with ancestral spirits, and receive guidance on matters of great importance to the individual or the community. Central to the Peyote Religion is the notion of the peyote as a "sacred medicine" rather than a recreational drug. It is regarded as a gift from the Creator and is treated with reverence and respect. Peyote ceremonies typically involve singing of hymns, led by a Roadman or ceremonial leader, who guides the participants through the ritual. The singing, accompanied by drumming and prayer, plays a necessary place in creating a sacred atmosphere and encouraging a sense of unity among the congregation. The Peyote Religion focuses on core values like humility, compassion, and harmony with the natural world. Participants seek healing, both physical and spiritual, and engage in self-reflection and personal growth during these ceremonies. The rituals serve as a means of strengthening cultural identity and preserving indigenous traditions, especially in the face of historical challenges and cultural assimilation.

The Native American Church played an important place in safeguarding the practice of Peyote Religion by advocating for legal protections to ensure the religious use of peyote. In 1978, the American Indian Religious Freedom Act was signed into law, affirming the right of Native Americans to use peyote in their religious ceremonies.

The Peyote Religion is a sacred tradition that revolves around the ceremonial use of the peyote cactus to facilitate spiritual communion and healing. It is a profound expression of indigenous spirituality, emphasizing reverence for the natural world, unity among practitioners, and a deep connection to ancestral traditions. Through its rituals, the Peyote Religion continues to provide spiritual guidance and encourage a sense of cultural identity and resilience among Native American communities.

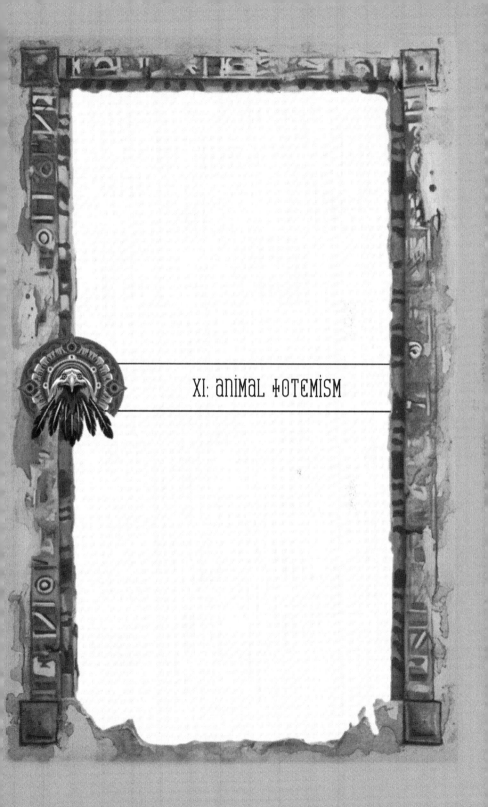

XI: Animal Totemism

Animal totemism is a profound belief system that centers on the concept of a spiritual connection or kinship between a human and a particular animal species. This ancient and cross-cultural belief holds that each individual has an animal spirit guide or totem animal that is intricately linked to their essence and life adventure. It is a belief that transcends geographical bounds and has been embraced by diverse indigenous cultures throughout history. At the core of animal totemism is the belief that animals possess unique qualities, characteristics, and symbolic meanings. Each animal species is seen as embodying specific traits, virtues, and wisdom that can offer guidance, protection, and insight to individuals who are spiritually connected to them. These totem animals are often regarded as spiritual allies and sources of encouragement.

The selection of one's totem animal is not arbitrary but is believed to be determined by a variety of factors, including one's birth date, personal experiences, dreams, and visions. Totem animals are often associated with a person's strengths, challenges, and life purpose. They serve as guides and teachers, helping individuals navigate their life's adventure and understand their place within the greater atlas of existence. Animal totemism is not limited to the physical world; it includes the spiritual and metaphysical dimensions as well. Individuals who get in touch with this belief often engage in rituals, ceremonies, and practices to connect with their totem animals. These rituals can include meditation, dreamwork, and shamanic journeys, where individuals seek direct communion with their animal spirit guides. Each totem animal carries its own unique symbolism and significance. For example, the wolf may symbolize courage, loyalty, and teamwork, while the owl is often associated with wisdom, intuition, and the mysteries of the night. The bear is often seen as a symbol of strength, healing, and introspection, while the butterfly stands for transformation and rebirth.

Animal totemism also focuses on the enmeshment of all living beings and the natural world. It underscores the idea that humans are not separate from the animal kingdom but are intricately linked to it. This belief encourages a sense of respect, reverence, and stewardship toward the environment and the creatures that inhabit it. Throughout history, various indigenous cultures, including Native American tribes, Aboriginal peoples of Australia, and African tribes, have practiced animal totemism as an integral part of their spiritual traditions. These totemic beliefs have played a central place in tribal rituals, storytelling, and the transmission of cultural wisdom from one generation to the next.

In contemporary times, the concept of animal totemism has resonated with individuals from diverse backgrounds seeking a deeper connection to nature, spirituality, and their own inner selves. It has found expression in practices like animal symbolism in art, literature, and modern forms of spiritual adventure.

Animal totemism is a belief system that recognizes the spiritual connection and kinship between humans and specific animal species. It offers individuals a profound scaffolding for understanding themselves, their strengths, and their life's adventure through the guidance and symbolism provided by their totem animals. This belief system celebrates the enmeshment of all living beings and the wisdom that can be gleaned from the natural world, emphasizing respect for both the animal kingdom and the environment as a whole.

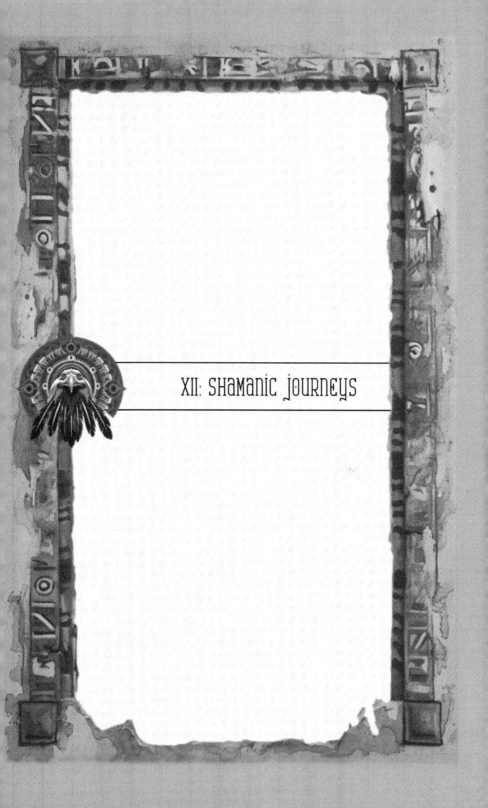

XII: SHAMANIC JOURNEYS

Shamanic journeys are profound spiritual practices that involve a shaman, a specially trained individual often regarded as a spiritual intermediary, entering altered states of consciousness to interact with the spiritual world. These journeys are central to shamanic traditions across various cultures and have been practiced for millennia. They are a means of seeking guidance, healing, and insight from the spiritual world and are characterized by their depth and transformative power. At the heart of shamanic journeys is the belief that the shaman can travel through the bounds between the ordinary, everyday reality and the hidden, spiritual worlds. The shaman achieves altered states of consciousness through various means, which may include rhythmic drumming, chanting, dancing, fasting, or the use of psychoactive substances. These altered states enable the shaman to access the spirit world, communicate with spirits, and perform acts of healing, divination, and soul retrieval.

Key elements of shamanic journeys include:

Spiritual Allies

Shamans often have spiritual allies or spirit guides that assist them during their journeys. These allies may take the form of animals, ancestors, or other beings and provide guidance and protection in the spiritual worlds.

Drumming and Chanting

Rhythmic drumming and chanting are common techniques used to induce altered states of consciousness. The repetitive sound and vibrations of the drum or chant can alter the shaman's perception and facilitate their adventure.

Soul Retrieval

Shamanic journeys may involve the retrieval of lost or fragmented aspects of the soul. It is believed that traumatic experiences can lead to soul loss, and the shaman's place is to retrieve these lost soul fragments to restore a person's wellness.

Healing and Divination

`Shamans use their journeys to diagnose and heal physical, emotional, and spiritual ailments. They may also seek insights into questions or challenges facing individuals or the community through divination techniques.

Communion with Nature

Many shamanic traditions emphasize a deep connection with the natural world. Shamans often adventure to connect with the spirits of animals, plants, and landscapes to gain knowledge and power.

Crossing the Threshold

During a shamanic adventure, the shaman metaphorically crosses a threshold or enters a portal to the spirit world. This threshold can be represented by a symbolic doorway, a tunnel, or other transitional elements.

Ecstasy and Transformation

Shamanic journeys can be intense and transformative experiences. They often involve a sense of ecstasy, as the shaman's consciousness transcends ordinary reality. These experiences can lead to personal growth, healing, and expanded spiritual awareness.

Shamanic traditions that incorporate journeying are found in various cultures around the world, including among indigenous peoples in North and South America, Siberia, Africa, and Asia. While the specific practices and beliefs may vary from one tradition to another, the core concept of the shamanic adventure as a vehicle for spiritual adventure and healing remains a common theme. In contemporary times, shamanic journeying has experienced a resurgence of interest among individuals seeking alternative spiritual and healing practices. Workshops, books, and guided meditation sessions often provide opportunities for people to adventure through shamanic journeying as a means of personal and spiritual growth.

Shamanic journeys are profound practices involving altered states of consciousness that enable shamans to interact with the spiritual world. These journeys are integral to shamanic traditions across cultures and serve as a means of healing, divination, and spiritual growth. They highlight the shaman's place as a bridge between the ordinary and spiritual worlds, emphasizing the enmeshment of all life and the potential for transformation and insight through communion with the spirit world.

XIII: False Face Society

The Iroquois False Face Society, deeply founded in the spiritual traditions of the Haudenosaunee, or Six Nations Confederacy, holds a sacred place in the opulent atlas of indigenous cultures in North America. This venerable society is renowned for its distinctive masks, carved from living trees, which are believed to embody powerful spirits and are used in healing rituals. The False Face Society's practices reflect a profound connection between the physical and spiritual worlds, offering insight into their belief system, medicinal knowledge, and the lasting heritage of their cultural traditions.

The Iroquois, also known as the Haudenosaunee, consist of six distinct but related nations: the Mohawk, Oneida, Onondaga, Cayuga, Seneca, and Tuscarora. These nations form a confederacy that traces its foundations back over a thousand years and is known for its sophisticated political structure, the Great Law of Peace, as well as its spiritual and healing traditions. The False Face Society is one of the most prominent healing societies among the Iroquois, and its practices are deeply ingrained in their cultural and spiritual heritage. At the heart of this society are the masks, which are regarded as both sacred objects and powerful healing tools. The masks are made from the wood of the basswood tree, carefully selected and carved by skilled artisans within the society.

One of the distinguishing features of these masks is their unique, grotesque appearance. They often depict distorted, exaggerated facial features, with deep furrows, bulging eyes, and grimacing expressions. The masks are intentionally crafted to appear unsettling and otherworldly, reflecting the belief that they embody spirits with the power to heal and protect. The spirits associated with the False Face masks are known as the "False Faces" or "Spirits of the Forest." These spirits are believed to reside within the living trees from which the masks are carved. When a tree is selected for mask-making, it is believed that the spirit residing in the tree willingly sacrifices itself to become part of the healing process. This symbiotic relationship between humans, trees, and spirits underscores the deep respect and reciprocity that permeate Iroquois spirituality. The False Face masks serve as vessels through which these healing spirits can interact with the physical world. When a member of the False Face Society wears one of these masks during a healing ritual, they are believed to become a conduit for the spirit's presence. The masks are respected as the physical embodiment of the spirit, and their power is harnessed to aid in the healing of the afflicted individual. The healing rituals conducted by the False Face Society are both spiritual and medicinal in nature. The society's members, often referred to as "medicine helpers" or "carriers of the masks," are specially trained individuals who undergo a rigorous initiation process to become adept at conducting these ceremonies. The rituals typically take place in a communal longhouse, a central gathering place for Iroquois communities.

One of the primary functions of the False Face Society is to address illnesses and ailments, both physical and spiritual, within the community. When someone falls ill, it is often believed to be a manifestation of disharmony or imbalance in their relationship with the spirit world. The False Face Society's healers diagnose the nature of the illness and prescribe specific rituals and treatments to restore harmony and wellness. During a healing ritual, the False Face mask is worn by a medicine helper who dances and performs various ceremonial actions. The mask is brought to life through the dance, with the medicine helper embodying the spirit's presence. The rattling of gourds, the chanting of healing songs, and the use of traditional medicines are integral elements of these ceremonies. One of the key features of these healing rituals is the use of tobacco, a sacred plant in many indigenous cultures. Tobacco is offered to the spirits as a sign of respect and gratitude. It is believed that the spirits favorably respond to the offering of tobacco, strengthening their connection with the mask-wearer and increasing the efficacy of the healing.

The healing process often involves the expulsion of malevolent spirits or negative forces that are causing the illness. The False Face mask, with its fearsome visage, is seen as a formidable presence that can intimidate and drive away these harmful entities. The medicine helper's dance and actions are intended to confront and challenge the source of the illness, ultimately leading to its expulsion from the afflicted individual.

The rituals of the False Face Society also incorporate the concept of "reciprocity," a fundamental principle in indigenous spirituality. It is believed that the healing spirits expect something in return for their assistance. In this spirit of reciprocity, community members offer gifts, often in the form of food or other provisions, to express gratitude for the healing received. In addition to addressing illnesses, the False Face Society is involved in other spiritual and community activities. They hold a place in ensuring the wellness and protection of the community by conducting rituals to ward off malevolent forces, promote fertility, and offer blessings for various occasions. The society is an integral part of the communal life of the Iroquois people, participating in ceremonies related to the changing of seasons, agricultural practices, and rites of passage.

The False Face Society is not limited to the physical world; it also has a spiritual dimension. It is believed that the society's members can enter into altered states of consciousness during their healing rituals, allowing them to communicate with the spirits more effectively. These altered states may be induced through fasting, chanting, and rhythmic drumming, providing a means of connecting with the spirit world. The masks themselves are respected as living beings with their own needs and requirements. They are cared for and ritually fed by the society's members. The wood of the masks is believed to continue to grow over time, requiring periodic maintenance and offerings to ensure the continued presence and vitality of the spirit within. The False Face Society is deeply charted with the broader cultural and spiritual map of the Iroquois people. Its practices reflect a holistic understanding of health, encompassing the physical, emotional, and spiritual aspects of wellness. The masks themselves are not static objects but dynamic vessels of spiritual power and transformation.

In closing, the Iroquois False Face Society is a venerable and deeply spiritual institution within the Haudenosaunee culture. Its distinctive masks, carved from living trees, are believed to embody healing spirits and are used in rituals that address physical and spiritual ailments. The society's practices reflect a profound connection between humans, nature, and the spirit world, emphasizing reciprocity, respect for the environment, and the lasting heritage of indigenous cultural traditions. The False Face Society stands as a confirmation of the resilience of indigenous spirituality and the profound wisdom it imparts to those who seek its healing and guidance.

XIV: POTLATCH CEREMONIES

Potlatch ceremonies, deeply embedded in the cultural map of the indigenous peoples of the Pacific Northwest Coast, constitute a complex and multifaceted tradition that includes feasting, dancing, and the redistribution of wealth. These elaborate and highly ritualized events hold immense significance within the social, economic, and spiritual worlds of the indigenous cultures in the region, reflecting complex systems of status, reciprocity, and community cohesion.

The term "potlatch" is derived from the Chinook Jargon word "patshatl," which means "to give away" or "a gift." However, the potlatch is far more than a mere gift-giving ceremony; it is a profound and complex cultural practice that serves various interconnected purposes within indigenous societies, like the Kwakwaka'wakw, Haida, Nuu-chah-nulth, Coast Salish, and other related groups. Central to the potlatch is the concept of wealth redistribution, but this wealth extends beyond material possessions to include prestige, honor, and status. Potlatches are often hosted by individuals or families of high social standing, who use these gatherings as an opportunity to demonstrate their generosity and elevate their status within the community. The act of giving away wealth, in various forms, symbolizes their prosperity and reinforces their position of leadership.

The elements and significance of potlatch ceremonies include:

Wealth Redistribution

Potlatches involve the distribution of a wide range of valuable items, including blankets, food, canoes, artwork, and ceremonial regalia. The wealth distributed during a potlatch acts as a form of social currency, enhancing the prestige of the host and strengthening social bonds within the community.

Status and Prestige

Hosting a potlatch is a way for individuals or families to demonstrate their status and leadership within the community. The scale and grandeur of the event often reflect the host's wealth and influence.

Ceremonial Dancing and Performances

Potlatch ceremonies feature elaborate dances, songs, and performances that are integral to the proceedings. These dances often recount historical events, convey spiritual messages, or tell stories of the host's lineage and achievements.

Ritual Feasting

Feasting is a central component of potlatch ceremonies, and it serves both practical and symbolic purposes. While guests enjoy a bountiful meal, the act of providing food also symbolizes the host's ability to care for and nourish the community.

Gift-Giving and Reciprocity

Potlatches are not one-sided acts of generosity; they are imbued with a strong sense of reciprocity. Guests who receive gifts are expected to reciprocate in the future, either through their own potlatch or other forms of support and assistance.

Cultural Transmission

Potlatch ceremonies serve as a means of passing down cultural knowledge, traditions, and stories. They are essential for maintaining the continuity of indigenous cultures and preserving ancestral teachings.

Life Cycle Events

Potlatches are often held to mark significant life events, like births, marriages, and deaths. These ceremonies help to anchor individuals within their communities and reinforce their cultural identity.

Spiritual Significance

Potlatch ceremonies have spiritual dimensions, involving the invocation of ancestral spirits and the seeking of blessings for the community. They are also a means of connecting with the natural world and the spiritual world.

Social Cohesion

Potlatches hold a necessary place in reinforcing social bonds within indigenous communities. These events bring people together, encouraging a sense of unity and collective identity.

Potlatch ceremonies have a long and complex history, and their practice was deeply affected by colonialism and government policies. In the late 19th and early 20th centuries, the Canadian and U.S. governments attempted to suppress potlatches, viewing them as wasteful and a threat to their assimilationist agenda. Potlatch bans were enforced through legislation, and indigenous peoples faced severe penalties for participating in these ceremonies. Despite these challenges, potlatches have endured and experienced a revitalization in recent decades. They continue to be celebrated by indigenous communities as a means of preserving their cultural heritage, asserting their identity, and strengthening their social bonds.

In conclusion, potlatch ceremonies are complex and multifunctional traditions that have played a central place in the indigenous cultures of the Pacific Northwest Coast. They include wealth redistribution, status elevation, cultural transmission, and spiritual significance. These ceremonies are a confirmation of the resilience and lasting vitality of indigenous cultures, as they continue to celebrate and uphold their traditions in the face of historical challenges and cultural change.

Potlatches are not just gatherings of celebration but also profound expressions of community, identity, and reciprocity within indigenous societies.

XV: GREEN CORN CEREMONY

The Green Corn Ceremony, a sacred and profound ritual, holds a central place among the indigenous tribes of the Southeastern United States, including the Creek, Cherokee, Seminole, Choctaw, and others. Founded in the spiritual and agricultural traditions of these peoples, the ceremony is celebrated as a time of renewal, purification, and communal unity, coinciding with the ripening of the corn harvest. The Green Corn Ceremony, known by various names among different tribes, is a multifaceted event that includes cultural, spiritual, and social dimensions, reflecting the deep connection between indigenous communities and the cycles of nature. At its core, the Green Corn Ceremony revolves around the harvesting and consumption of fresh, tender corn, a staple crop of the Southeastern tribes. The ceremony typically takes place during the late summer months when the corn has reached its peak of ripeness and flavor. While the specific timing and details of the ceremony may vary among tribes, several overarching themes and elements are common to most Green Corn Ceremonies.

Renewal and Purification

The Green Corn Ceremony is often seen as a time of cleansing and renewal, both for individuals and the community as a whole. It is an opportunity to rid oneself of negative influences, illness, and misfortunes from the past year, and to start anew with a fresh, clean slate. This theme of renewal is symbolized by the fresh corn, which stands for the vitality of life and the promise of a new beginning.

Spiritual Significance

The ceremony is deeply intertwined with the spiritual beliefs of the Southeastern tribes. It is a time for giving thanks to the Creator and the spirits for the bountiful harvest and for the continued wellness of the community. Ceremonial leaders, often known as "corn priests" or "medicine people," hold an important place in conducting rituals, offering prayers, and ensuring the proper observance of sacred traditions.

Ritual Preparations

Leading up to the Green Corn Ceremony, extensive preparations are made. Participants fast, cleanse themselves through bathing or sweat lodge ceremonies, and abstain from certain activities and foods. These preparations serve to purify the body and spirit, ensuring that participants approach the ceremony with reverence and a clear mind.

Feasting and Sharing

The heart of the Green Corn Ceremony is the communal feast. Freshly harvested corn, along with other foods like beans, squash, and various meats, is prepared and shared among the participants. The act of eating the fresh corn is symbolic of absorbing the vitality and blessings of the Earth and the Creator. Sharing food encourages a sense of unity and reciprocity within the community.

Dancing and Singing

Dance and song are integral components of the Green Corn Ceremony. Participants engage in traditional dances and sing songs that have been passed down through generations. These dances often feature complex footwork and colorful regalia. The rhythms of the drum and the melodies of the songs are believed to invoke the spirits and facilitate communication with the divine.

Ceremonial Fire

A sacred fire, kindled for the ceremony, is tended throughout the event. It stands for the presence of the Creator and the lasting spiritual connection between the people and the natural world. Participants often make offerings to the fire as a sign of their gratitude and respect.

Social Reunion

Beyond its spiritual and ceremonial aspects, the Green Corn Ceremony acts as a social and cultural gathering. It provides an opportunity for people to come together, strengthen bonds, and pass on traditional knowledge to younger generations. It is a time for storytelling, teaching, and the transmission of cultural values.

Symbolism of Corn

Corn holds immense symbolic significance within the Green Corn Ceremony. It is respected as a sacred gift from the Creator, providing sustenance and spiritual nourishment. The different colors of corn, like white, yellow, and blue, are associated with specific spiritual qualities and attributes.

The Green Corn Ceremony is not a monolithic event; rather, it exhibits variations in customs, rituals, and practices among different tribes. Each tribe brings its unique cultural elements and interpretations to the ceremony, reflecting the diversity of indigenous traditions within the Southeastern region. For example, the Creek people refer to the ceremony as "Busk," while the Cherokee call it "Selu," and the Seminole refer to it as "Ee-lon-gee-thlo." In addition to its spiritual and cultural significance, the Green Corn Ceremony has faced challenges and disruptions throughout history. The arrival of European settlers and the imposition of colonial policies had a profound effect on indigenous practices, including the suppression of traditional ceremonies. Despite these challenges, many Southeastern tribes have persisted in preserving and revitalizing their cultural heritage, including the Green Corn Ceremony. Today, the Green Corn Ceremony continues to be celebrated among various Southeastern tribes as a confirmation of the resilience and endurance of indigenous cultures.

Efforts to revitalize and pass on these traditions to younger generations hold a necessary place in preserving the opulent atlas of indigenous heritage in the United States. The ceremony acts as a living confirmation of the deep connection between indigenous communities and the land, as well as their lasting commitment to the cycles of renewal and purification that have sustained their cultures for generations.

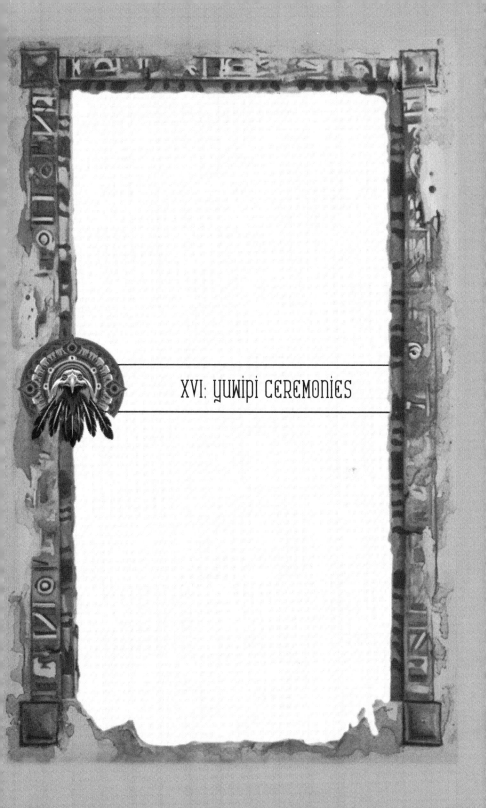

XVI: YUWIPI CEREMONIES

Yuwipi ceremonies, originating from the Lakota Sioux tradition, are profound and sacred healing rituals that invoke spiritual powers to address physical, emotional, and spiritual ailments within the community. These ceremonies are characterized by their complex and mysterious nature, involving a ceremonial bundle, a sacred song, and a ritualist known as the yuwipi man or woman who performs the ceremony. Yuwipi ceremonies are deeply founded in Lakota spirituality and are regarded as a means of connecting with the spirit world to bring about healing, guidance, and balance.

The term "yuwipi" itself is derived from the Lakota language and can be translated to mean "to bind" or "to tie up." This reflects the fundamental aspect of the ceremony where the yuwipi practitioner is bound or tied with cords or ropes, securing them to a structure or support within the sacred space. This binding is symbolic of the connection between the physical and spiritual worlds and the practitioner's place as a conduit between the two.

Preparation and Ritual Space
The preparation for a yuwipi ceremony is a careful process that begins with the selection of a suitable location, often within a specially constructed sacred enclosure or tipi. The sacred space is carefully arranged and decorated, with various symbolic items and offerings placed within

it. The ceremonial bundle, also known as the "yuwipi bundle" or "medicine bundle," plays a central place and contains sacred objects, herbs, and items of spiritual significance.

Prior to the ceremony, the yuwipi practitioner undergoes a period of fasting, prayer, and purification. This preparation is essential to attune the practitioner's spirit to the energies of the ceremony and ensure their readiness to serve as a vessel for the healing spirits. The practitioner's state of mind and spiritual alignment are of utmost importance in the success of the ceremony.

The Ceremony Itself

The heart of the yuwipi ceremony is the binding and following trance-like state of the practitioner. The practitioner is typically bound with a series of cords or ropes, securing them to a central support or frame within the ceremonial space. The binding process is performed with great care and precision, as it is believed to establish a connection between the practitioner and the spirit world.

Once bound, the yuwipi practitioner enters a deep altered state of consciousness. This altered state is achieved through a combination of fasting, rhythmic chanting, drumming, and the invocation of sacred songs. The practitioner's sensory perception is heightened, and they become receptive to spiritual energies and messages from the spirit world.

117

Throughout the ceremony, participants gather in the sacred space, creating an atmosphere of reverence and focused intent. They may offer prayers, sing sacred songs, and provide support to the practitioner. The presence of the community is seen as essential, as their collective energy and intentions enhance the ceremony's effectiveness. The yuwipi practitioner's trance state allows them to commune with the spirit world and seek guidance and healing on behalf of individuals who come to the ceremony with specific ailments or concerns. The practitioner may use divination tools or objects from the ceremonial bundle to interpret messages from the spirits. These messages can pertain to the causes of illness, the remedies needed, or insights into personal challenges.

Healing and Guidance

Yuwipi ceremonies are often searched out for healing purposes, addressing physical, emotional, or spiritual imbalances. The healing methods employed can vary, depending on the guidance received from the spirits. This may include the use of traditional medicines, energy work, or other forms of spiritual intervention. The practitioner acts as a conduit for the healing energies channeled from the spirit world to the individual in need.

The yuwipi ceremony is not limited to healing but may also include seeking guidance and wisdom for personal or communal matters.

Participants may come with questions about their life path, relationships, or broader community concerns. The ceremony provides a means of accessing spiritual insights and solutions to these issues.

Yuwipi ceremonies are a confirmation of the deep spiritual traditions and healing practices of the Lakota Sioux and related indigenous communities. These rituals, with their complex symbolism and profound symbolism, are a means of bridging the physical and spiritual worlds. The practitioner's trance state and communication with the spirit world offer a path to healing, guidance, and transformation. While yuwipi ceremonies are deeply founded in Lakota culture, they have also gained recognition and respect beyond indigenous communities. Many individuals from diverse backgrounds seek out these ceremonies as a means of addressing physical and emotional challenges, seeking spiritual growth, and connecting with the profound wisdom of indigenous traditions. In essence, yuwipi ceremonies represent a living expression of the enmeshment of all life and the belief in the power of the spirit world to bring healing and balance to the physical world. They are a confirmation of the lasting vitality of indigenous spiritual practices and their capacity to offer solace, guidance, and transformation to those who seek their wisdom.

XVII: BLACK DRINK CEREMONY

The Black Drink Ceremony, a sacred and ancient ritual practiced by various Southeastern Native American tribes, is a purification ceremony that involves the consumption of a caffeine-opulent, emetic ceremonial drink known as "Black Drink." This tradition is deeply founded in the cultural and spiritual map of indigenous communities like the Choctaw, Creek, Seminole, and Cherokee, among others. The Black Drink Ceremony acts as a means of cleansing the body and spirit, promoting communal unity, and connecting with the natural and spiritual worlds.

Origin and Significance

The origins of the Black Drink Ceremony can be traced back thousands of years, reflecting the deep history and cultural continuity of indigenous peoples in the Southeastern United States. Archaeological evidence suggests that this ritual was practiced by prehistoric Native American societies long before the arrival of European settlers. The tradition has endured through generations, maintaining its spiritual and cultural significance. At its core, the Black Drink Ceremony is a purification ritual. It is typically conducted in the context of important communal events, like tribal gatherings, councils, initiations, and warrior ceremonies. The Black Drink itself, made from the leaves of the yaupon holly (Ilex vomitoria) and sometimes mixed with other herbs, acts as a potent symbol of purification and renewal.

The Black Drink is notable for its caffeine content, which can be much higher than that of coffee or tea. Consumed in significant quantities during the ceremony, it has a stimulating effect that induces vomiting, an important aspect of the purification process. The emetic properties of the drink are believed to cleanse the body of impurities and promote spiritual clarity.

Preparation and Ritual Space

The preparation for a Black Drink Ceremony is a careful process that involves the gathering and preparation of the yaupon holly leaves. These leaves are typically harvested and dried in advance, and their preparation is carried out with great care and reverence. The ceremonial space is selected and arranged to create an atmosphere of sacredness, often in a communal gathering area or ceremonial ground.

The Ceremony Itself

The Black Drink Ceremony is a communal event, and its participants gather to partake in the ritual. The ceremony is led by a designated ritualist or spiritual leader, who plays a central place in guiding the proceedings. The specific rituals and customs associated with the Black Drink Ceremony may vary among tribes, but several overarching elements are common to most ceremonies.

Preparation and Fasting

Participants often undergo a period of fasting and purification leading up to the ceremony. This involves abstaining from food and drink, as well as other physical and spiritual preparations, to ready themselves for the purification process.

Consumption of the Black Drink

The central act of the ceremony involves the consumption of the Black Drink. Participants drink the beverage, often in measured quantities, to induce vomiting. The vomiting is seen as a necessary and cleansing part of the process, ridding the body of impurities and promoting spiritual clarity.

Song and Chant

Singing and chanting are integral to the Black Drink Ceremony. Participants engage in traditional songs and chants that have been passed down through generations. These songs often convey spiritual messages, invoke the spirits, and facilitate a sense of unity and connection among the participants.

Prayer and Reflection

Prayer is an important aspect of the ceremony, with participants offering their intentions and gratitude to the Creator and the spirits. The Black Drink Ceremony is a time for personal reflection, seeking guidance, and connecting with the natural and spiritual worlds.

Communal Bonding
Beyond its spiritual significance, the Black Drink Ceremony encourages communal bonding and unity. It is an opportunity for participants to come together, share in a sacred experience, and strengthen their sense of belonging within the tribal community.

Symbolism of the Yaupon Holly
The yaupon holly, from which the Black Drink is made, holds deep symbolism within the ceremony. It is seen as a sacred plant, embodying the spirit of purification and renewal. The plant's caffeine content, along with its emetic properties, is regarded as a gift from the Creator for the wellness of the people.

Spiritual and Healing Aspects
The Black Drink Ceremony serves multiple spiritual and healing purposes within indigenous communities. It is believed to cleanse both the physical body and the spirit, promoting physical health and emotional wellness. The act of vomiting is seen as a means of purging negative energies and restoring harmony within the individual.

Additionally, the ceremony offers a space for seeking guidance and insight. Participants may come to the ceremony with questions, seeking spiritual clarity or direction in their lives. The heightened state of consciousness induced by the Black Drink is believed to facilitate a closer connection with the spirit world and the reception of messages from the Creator and ancestral spirits.

Challenges and Resilience

Throughout history, the practice of the Black Drink Ceremony faced challenges and suppression, particularly during the era of European colonization and the imposition of colonial policies. These policies often searched out to suppress indigenous cultural and spiritual practices, viewing them as a threat to colonial control. Despite these challenges, many indigenous communities have persevered in preserving and revitalizing their cultural heritage, including the Black Drink Ceremony.

Today, the tradition continues to be celebrated among various Southeastern tribes as a confirmation of the resilience and endurance of indigenous cultures. Efforts to revitalize and pass on these traditions to younger generations hold a necessary place in preserving the opulent atlas of indigenous heritage in the United States.

In conclusion, the Black Drink Ceremony is a sacred and ancient ritual of purification and renewal practiced by various Southeastern Native

American tribes. It is deeply founded in the cultural and spiritual traditions of these indigenous communities and reflects their lasting connection with the natural and spiritual worlds. The ceremony, with its symbolic use of the Black Drink and the act of vomiting, acts as a means of cleansing the body and spirit, promoting physical and spiritual wellness, and encouraging communal unity. It stands as a living confirmation of the profound wisdom and resilience of indigenous cultures in the face of historical challenges and cultural change.

XVIII: TOLTEC CIVILIZATION

The influence of the ancient Toltec civilization on the spirituality and practices of Southwestern tribes stands for a complex and multifaceted historical interaction. The Toltecs, known for their advanced knowledge in various fields, including architecture, astronomy, and art, had a significant presence in Mesoamerica, particularly in the region now encompassing central Mexico, starting from the 9th to the 12th centuries. Over time, their influence radiated outward, reaching the Southwestern United States and impacting the indigenous tribes residing there, including the Pueblo, Hopi, and Zuni peoples. This influence primarily occurred through trade, cultural exchange, and migration, leading to the incorporation of certain elements of Toltec spirituality and practices into the belief systems of Southwestern tribes.

Trade and Cultural Exchange

One of the primary avenues through which Toltec influence reached the Southwestern tribes was trade and cultural exchange. The ancient trade routes of Mesoamerica extended northward, connecting the Toltec civilization with various indigenous groups in the American Southwest. Through these trade networks, ideas, religious beliefs, and material culture were exchanged. The exchange of goods and knowledge encouraged an opulent cultural milieu in which elements of Toltec spirituality and practices intermingled with those of the Southwestern tribes.

Architectural and Artistic Influence

The Toltecs were renowned for their architectural achievements and artistic expressions. Notable Toltec architectural features, like pyramid-temples and ball courts, have been identified in Mesoamerican sites. Elements of Toltec architectural design and artistic motifs are found in the Southwestern tribal regions, particularly in the Pueblo communities. The incorporation of certain architectural and artistic elements into Pueblo structures and pottery reflects the cross-cultural exchange that took place.

Agricultural Practices

The Toltecs, like many indigenous cultures, were skilled agriculturalists. They developed advanced farming techniques, including terraced agriculture, which allowed for efficient food production. These agricultural practices influenced the Southwestern tribes in terms of farming methods, crop cultivation, and water management. The adoption of certain agricultural techniques contributed to the sustainability of farming in the arid Southwestern landscapes.

Cosmology and Astronomy

The Toltecs had a sophisticated understanding of astronomy and cosmology, and their observations of celestial bodies played a significant place in their religious and calendrical systems. Southwestern tribes, like the Hopi, also had well-developed astronomical traditions, which may have been influenced by Mesoamerican knowledge. The incorporation of celestial observations into religious ceremonies, calendar systems, and the tracking of seasonal changes may have been influenced by Toltec cosmological concepts.

Religious Syncretism

Toltec spirituality and religious practices exhibited syncretic elements that incorporated aspects of earlier Mesoamerican cultures, like the Maya and Teotihuacan. These syncretic features likely contributed to the adaptability of Toltec religious ideas when interacting with Southwestern tribes. Aspects of Toltec religious beliefs, including reverence for certain deities and sacred rituals, may have been incorporated into the spiritual practices of Southwestern tribes, enriching their own belief systems.

Oral Traditions and Storytelling

Oral traditions played a significant place in the transmission of cultural knowledge among indigenous tribes. Stories and legends passed down through generations may have contained elements influenced by interactions with other cultures, including the Toltecs. Mythological narratives, cosmogonic stories, and origin tales may reflect the intercultural exchange and the incorporation of Toltec themes into the narratives of Southwestern tribes.

Ritual Practices

Certain ritual practices and ceremonies among Southwestern tribes exhibit similarities to those of Mesoamerican cultures, including the Toltecs. Rituals related to agricultural cycles, seasonal changes, and celestial events may have been influenced by Toltec concepts. The use of ceremonial masks, sacred dances, and offerings to deities may have been adapted from Mesoamerican models, demonstrating the cultural blending that occurred over time.

Symbolism and Iconography

Symbolism and iconography are essential components of indigenous spirituality and artistic expression. The Toltecs, known for their complex symbolic systems, influenced the iconography used by Southwestern tribes in various contexts, like pottery, textiles, and petroglyphs. Shared symbols and motifs reflect the blending of cultural elements and the lasting effect of Toltec influence on the artistic and spiritual expressions of Southwestern tribes.

Migration and Ancestral Connections

The movement of populations, including tribal groups, across regions contributed to the dissemination of cultural elements and practices. Some Southwestern tribes may have ancestral connections or migration histories that link them to Mesoamerican regions where Toltec influence was prominent. These connections could have facilitated the exchange of ideas, beliefs, and practices between the two regions. The effect of the ancient Toltec civilization on the spirituality and practices of Southwestern tribes stands for a complex and nuanced historical interaction. While direct historical evidence of Toltec influence in the American Southwest is limited, the presence of shared elements in various aspects of culture, including architecture, agriculture, cosmology, and symbolism, suggests a meaningful cultural exchange. The lasting heritage of this interaction is evident in the cultural richness and diversity of Southwestern indigenous traditions, where elements of Toltec spirituality and practices are charted with the unique belief systems of each tribe.

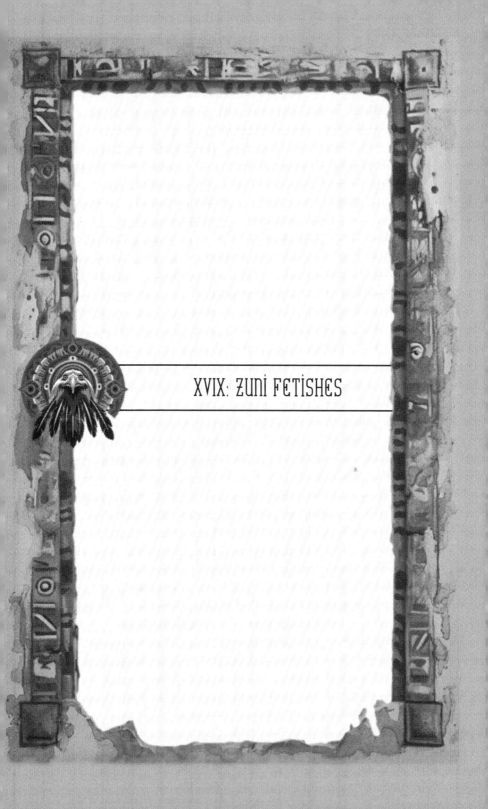

XVIX: ZUNI FETISHES

Zuni fetishes, small carvings carefully crafted from a variety of materials, are revered objects within the spiritual and cultural traditions of the Zuni people, a Native American tribe residing in the Southwestern United States. These fetishes are much more than mere works of art; they hold profound significance in Zuni religion, cosmology, and everyday life. Zuni fetishes are believed to possess protective and healing powers, serving as intermediaries between the spiritual world and the physical world, as well as symbols of the tribe's deep connection to the natural world.

Origins and Materials

The tradition of Zuni fetishes has ancient foundations, dating back hundreds of years. These sacred objects are crafted from various materials, with the most common being stone, including materials like serpentine, travertine, and alabaster. Fetishes can also be carved from other materials like wood, antler, shell, and more recently, minerals like turquoise. The choice of material is significant, as each type of stone or material is believed to carry specific spiritual properties.

Spiritual Significance

Zuni fetishes are central to the tribe's spiritual beliefs and practices. They are regarded as living beings with unique spirits or essences. In Zuni cosmology, all elements of the natural world, including animals, plants, and stones, possess spiritual energy. Fetishes are seen as vessels through which this energy can be channeled and harnessed for various purposes.

Animal Symbolism

A prominent aspect of Zuni fetishes is their depiction of animals. Each animal has its own unique symbolism and spiritual attributes. For example, the bear is associated with healing and strength, while the wolf stands for loyalty and family bonds. The eagle is revered for its connection to the sky and the Creator. The choice of animal and the way it is carved often reflects the intended purpose of the fetish.

Guardians and Guides

Zuni fetishes are believed to serve as protectors and guides for individuals. A person may have one or more personal fetishes that are chosen or given to them based on their individual spiritual needs. These personal fetishes are carried or worn as amulets and are thought to provide protection, guidance, and assistance on life's adventure.

Ritual Use

Fetishes are used in various Zuni ceremonies and rituals. They hold an important place in the tribe's religious practices, including the Kachina dances and the Shalako festival. During these ceremonies, fetishes are often carried, displayed, or incorporated into the rituals to invoke the spiritual energies associated with the animals they represent.

Healing and Medicine

Zuni fetishes are used in healing practices within the tribe. A Zuni medicine man or woman may employ fetishes as part of a healing ceremony to address physical, emotional, or spiritual ailments. The fetishes are seen as conduits for the transfer of healing energy.

Collecting and Trading

Beyond their spiritual significance, Zuni fetishes have gained recognition in the art world. Collectors and enthusiasts value these carvings for their craftsmanship and cultural significance. Zuni artists are renowned for their complex and detailed carvings, and fetishes are often collected and traded both within and outside the tribe.

The Place of the Carver

The creation of Zuni fetishes is a specialized skill passed down through generations. Skilled carvers, often from families with a long tradition of fetish carving, hold a necessary place in the creation of these objects. The carver must have a deep understanding of the spiritual attributes associated with each animal and material.

The Zuni Way of Life

Zuni fetishes are deeply integrated into the daily life of the tribe. They are not simply objects of religious reverence but are also part of everyday activities. Fetishes may be carried by individuals as personal totems, given as gifts to express sentiments, or used as teaching tools to impart cultural and spiritual knowledge to younger generations.

Respect for the Natural World

The creation and use of Zuni fetishes reflect the tribe's profound respect for the natural world. Zuni spirituality focuses on the enmeshment of all living beings and the importance of living in harmony with nature. Fetishes are a tangible expression of this worldview, serving as reminders of the tribe's close relationship with the animals and elements of the natural world.

Zuni fetishes are sacred objects that hold a central place in the spiritual and cultural life of the Zuni people. These small carvings made from various materials are imbued with spiritual energy and are believed to possess protective and healing powers. They serve as intermediaries between the physical and spiritual worlds, embodying the tribe's deep connection to the natural world and the animals that inhabit it. Zuni fetishes are a confirmation of the lasting vitality of indigenous traditions and the profound wisdom embedded within their cultural practices.

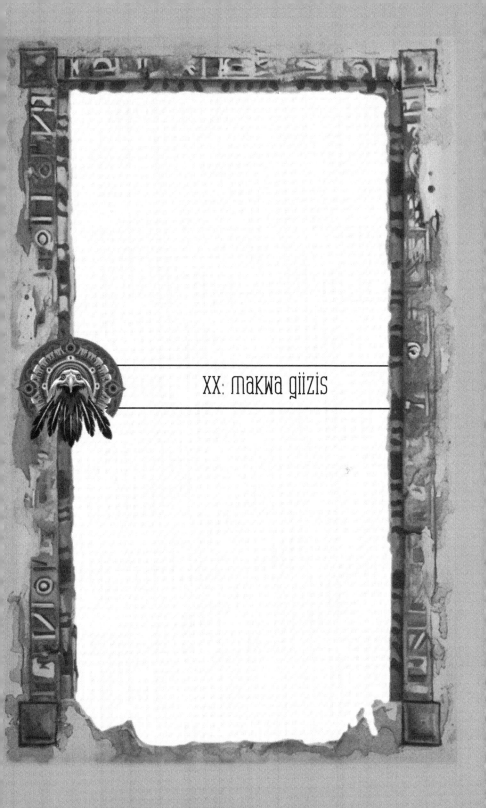

xx: makwa giizis

The Ojibwe, also known as the Anishinaabe or Chippewa, are a Native American tribe with an opulent cultural heritage that includes unique practices and interpretations of vision quests. The vision quest, or "makwa giizis" in the Ojibwe language, is a profound and sacred rite of passage for individuals seeking spiritual guidance, personal revelation, and a deeper connection with the spirit world. Ojibwe vision quests are deeply founded in their cultural and spiritual traditions, reflecting a distinctive approach to this ancient practice.

Spiritual Foundation

The Ojibwe vision quest is grounded in the tribe's spiritual beliefs and cosmology. Central to their worldview is the understanding of the enmeshment of all living beings and the importance of maintaining harmony with the natural and spiritual worlds. The vision quest is seen as a means of attaining spiritual insight and wisdom, allowing individuals to receive guidance from the spirit world.

Preparation and Mentorship

Before beginning on a vision quest, Ojibwe individuals undergo a period of preparation that includes fasting, purification, and reflection. They seek guidance from spiritual mentors, often referred to as "Mide" or "Medicine People," who provide support and guidance throughout the process. The mentor plays an important place in helping the quester interpret their visions and understand their significance.

Sacred Locations

Ojibwe vision quests are typically conducted at sacred locations within the tribe's traditional territories. These locations are chosen for their spiritual significance and connection to the spirit world. Common sites include remote wilderness areas, lakeshores, and isolated islands. The natural environment is respected as an essential aspect of the vision quest, as it facilitates a deeper connection with the spirits of the land.

Ritual and Ceremony

The vision quest itself involves a series of rituals and ceremonies. Questers often construct a small, temporary shelter or "miichim," where they will spend their time in isolation. The construction of the miichim is a ceremonial act, with specific protocols and prayers observed. Sacred objects, like feathers, tobacco, and medicines, are used as offerings and aids in connecting with the spirit world.

Fasting and Solitude

During the vision quest, individuals typically engage in a period of fasting and solitude that can last for several days or even weeks. Fasting is seen as a means of purifying the body and spirit, allowing the quester to become more receptive to spiritual visions and messages. Solitude in the wilderness encourages a profound sense of communion with nature and the spirits.

Seeking Visions

The central objective of the Ojibwe vision quest is to seek visions or spiritual experiences that offer guidance and insight. These visions can take various forms, like encounters with animal spirits, messages from ancestors, or insights into one's life path and purpose. The quester remains open to the guidance of the spirits and awaits these visions with humility and patience.

Interpretation and Integration

Once the vision quest is completed, the quester returns to the community and seeks the guidance of their mentor in interpreting the experiences and visions received during their time in isolation. The mentor helps the individual understand the significance of their visions and how to integrate them into their life and spiritual path. Visions are often regarded as personal medicine and are used for healing, guidance, and spiritual growth.

Community Involvement

The Ojibwe vision quest is not solely an individual endeavor; it also has a communal dimension. The quester's return to the community is marked by a welcoming ceremony, where the visions and insights gained are shared with the tribe. This communal aspect underscores the enmeshment of the Ojibwe people and their reliance on the wisdom and guidance received through vision quests to maintain the wellness of the community.

Contemporary Relevance

While Ojibwe vision quests are deeply founded in tradition, they remain relevant in contemporary times. Many Ojibwe individuals continue to undertake vision quests as a means of seeking guidance, healing, and personal transformation. The practice acts as a bridge between the ancestral wisdom of the Ojibwe and the challenges and opportunities of the modern world.

Cultural Preservation

The preservation of Ojibwe vision quests is essential for maintaining the tribe's cultural and spiritual heritage. Efforts are made to pass down the knowledge and rituals associated with vision quests to younger generations, ensuring that this sacred practice continues to thrive and evolve within the Ojibwe community.

In summary, the Ojibwe vision quest is a profound and sacred practice deeply embedded in the tribe's cultural and spiritual traditions. It reflects the Ojibwe worldview, emphasizing the enmeshment of all living beings and the importance of seeking guidance from the spirit world. The vision quest process involves rigorous preparation, solitude in the wilderness, and a deep communion with nature and the spirits. Visions received during these quests are regarded as sources of wisdom, healing, and personal guidance, and they are integrated into the individual's life and shared with the community. The practice continues to hold a necessary place in the spiritual and cultural life of the Ojibwe people, bridging the ancient traditions of their ancestors with the challenges of the modern world.

XXI: APACHE SUNRISE CEREMONY

The Apache Sunrise Ceremony, also known as the Na'ii'ees or Apache Puberty Ceremony, is a deeply significant and transformative rite of passage for young Apache girls as they transition from childhood to womanhood. This sacred ceremony holds immense cultural and spiritual significance within the Apache community and is a reflection of the tribe's opulent cultural heritage. The Apache Sunrise Ceremony is a comprehensive and elaborate event that involves various rituals, teachings, and cultural expressions, all aimed at preparing and empowering young Apache girls for their roles as women within the tribe.

Cultural Context and Significance

The Apache people, who reside in the Southwestern United States, have a distinct cultural identity characterized by their close connection to the land, their opulent oral traditions, and their profound respect for the natural world. The Sunrise Ceremony is a manifestation of Apache cultural values, emphasizing the importance of family, community, and the continuation of tribal traditions. It marks the moment when young girls are respected as young women and are entrusted with the responsibilities and knowledge necessary to contribute to their community's wellness.

Preparation and Mentorship

The preparation for the Apache Sunrise Ceremony begins years in advance. Young girls, typically around the age of puberty, are mentored by elder women and female relatives who guide them through the process. These mentors hold a critical place in teaching the girls about Apache culture, traditions, and the significance of the ceremony. They impart essential life skills, cultural knowledge, and spiritual teachings to prepare the girls for their transition into womanhood.

Spiritual Connection

Spirituality is at the core of the Apache Sunrise Ceremony. Apache belief systems are deeply founded in the spiritual connection between the people and the natural world. The ceremony is an opportunity for the girls to deepen their spiritual understanding and connection to the Apache deities, the Earth, and the ancestors. They learn about the sacredness of life and the importance of maintaining balance and harmony within themselves and their community.

Symbolism and Rituals

The Apache Sunrise Ceremony is marked by a series of symbolic rituals and practices. One of the most famous aspects is the elaborate and colorful attire worn by the girls, which includes traditional Apache dresses, jewelry, and headdresses. The girls also participate in dances, songs, and chants that are specific to the ceremony. The precise rituals may vary among Apache bands and communities, but common elements include the painting of the girls' bodies with sacred symbols and the offering of prayers and blessings.

Symbolism of the Sunrise

The Sunrise Ceremony derives its name from the symbolism of the rising sun, representing the new beginning and the dawning of a new phase in the girls' lives. The sun is seen as a source of light, energy, and guidance, which parallels the place of elders and mentors in providing guidance and wisdom to the girls.

Teaching and Education

Throughout the ceremony, the girls receive teachings and lessons from their mentors and elders. These teachings include a wide range of topics, including Apache history, traditions, family roles, and responsibilities as women. The girls are encouraged to ask questions and seek understanding as they begin on their adventure into womanhood.

Community Involvement

The Apache Sunrise Ceremony is a communal event that brings together family members, friends, and community members to celebrate and support the girls' transition. The community plays an active place in the ceremony, offering their blessings, prayers, and encouragement to the young girls. This collective involvement reinforces the sense of belonging and enmeshment within the Apache community.

Empowerment and Resilience

The Apache Sunrise Ceremony is not just a celebration of womanhood but also an empowerment ritual. It instills in the girls a sense of self-worth, resilience, and strength. They are taught to get in touch with their roles as future leaders, caregivers, and cultural bearers within the Apache community. This empowerment is necessary in helping young Apache women navigate the challenges they may encounter in life.

Passing on Traditions

One of the primary purposes of the Sunrise Ceremony is to ensure the continuity of Apache traditions and cultural knowledge. Through this rite of passage, the girls become carriers of their tribe's heritage, responsible for passing down the teachings, stories, and values to future generations. The ceremony is a living expression of the tribe's commitment to preserving their cultural identity.

Contemporary Relevance

The Apache Sunrise Ceremony remains a necessary and living tradition within Apache communities, adapting to contemporary contexts while retaining its core cultural and spiritual elements. Despite the challenges of modern life, the ceremony continues to thrive, providing young Apache girls with a strong foundation in their cultural heritage and a sense of pride in their identity as Apache women.

The Apache Sunrise Ceremony is a profound rite of passage that embodies the cultural and spiritual richness of the Apache people. It marks the transition of young girls into womanhood, imparting cultural knowledge, spiritual wisdom, and a sense of empowerment. This sacred ceremony acts as a confirmation of the lasting strength of Apache traditions, emphasizing the importance of community, spirituality, and the preservation of cultural heritage.

XXII: CROW DOG'S CASE

Crow Dog's Case, also known as Ex parte Crow Dog, is a landmark legal case in the United States that revolved around issues of Native American religious freedom and the practice of the Ghost Dance. It marked a critical moment in the ongoing struggle for Native American rights and sovereignty in the late 19th century. The case centered on the actions of a Brulé Lakota Sioux named Crow Dog, who was accused of murdering another Native American, Spotted Tail, on the Pine Ridge Indian Reservation in South Dakota in 1881. The case raised complex questions about tribal sovereignty, federal jurisdiction, and the protection of religious practices, ultimately highlighting the clash between Native American traditions and the legal scaffolding imposed by the U.S. government.

Historical Background

To understand the significance of Crow Dog's Case, it is essential to grasp the broader historical context in which it occurred. In the late 19th century, the United States government had been pursuing a policy of assimilation and control over Native American tribes, which often involved restricting indigenous religious practices and traditional ways of life. The Ghost Dance movement had emerged among various Plains tribes as a response to the profound social and spiritual upheaval brought about by colonization, displacement, and cultural disruption.

The Ghost Dance Movement

The Ghost Dance was a spiritual and cultural revival movement that emerged among Native American tribes, including the Lakota Sioux, in the late 19th century. The movement was founded by Wovoka (also known as Jack Wilson), a Paiute prophet who claimed to have received a vision from the spirit world. He preached that by performing the Ghost Dance, Native Americans could reunite with their ancestors, rid themselves of the influence of white settlers, and ultimately restore their traditional way of life.

The Ghost Dance quickly gained popularity among Plains tribes, and it was seen as a source of hope and spiritual renewal during a time of profound suffering and despair. However, U.S. government officials, including Indian agents, were deeply concerned about the movement, viewing it as a potential source of resistance and unrest among Native American populations.

The Murder of Spotted Tail

In 1881, Crow Dog, a respected Brulé Lakota Sioux leader, shot and killed Spotted Tail, another prominent Lakota leader, on the Pine Ridge Indian Reservation in South Dakota. The reasons for the murder were complex, involving personal disputes, tribal politics, and cultural clashes. Spotted Tail was perceived as cooperating with the U.S. government,

which led to tensions within the Lakota community. Crow Dog was arrested and tried for the murder of Spotted Tail, but the case quickly evolved into a legal and political quagmire that raised fundamental questions about tribal sovereignty, federal jurisdiction, and the protection of religious practices.

The Legal Battle

The trial of Crow Dog brought into focus the conflicting legal frameworks governing Native American tribes and the United States government. Crow Dog was tried in a federal court under U.S. law, but he argued that the murder had occurred within the bounds of the Pine Ridge Indian Reservation and should therefore be subject to tribal jurisdiction.

The case attracted significant attention, both nationally and internationally, as it raised important issues related to indigenous rights, tribal sovereignty, and the place of federal authority. Key figures, including prominent Native American leaders and advocates, became involved in the legal battle.

The Supreme Court Decision

In 1883, Crow Dog's case reached the U.S. Supreme Court, which issued a landmark decision in Ex parte Crow Dog. In a unanimous ruling, the Court held that federal courts did not have jurisdiction over crimes committed by one Native

American against another on tribal land. The decision was based on the interpretation of the 1868 Treaty of Fort Laramie, which had established the bounds of the Lakota Sioux reservations and their right to self-governance. The Supreme Court's decision, while significant in recognizing tribal sovereignty and jurisdiction, did not result in Crow Dog's immediate release. Instead, he was held by the federal authorities until he received a presidential pardon in 1885. Crow Dog's case had a lasting effect on the legal status of Native American tribes and their right to govern themselves within their territories.

Implications and Heritage

Crow Dog's Case had several far-reaching implications for Native American rights and the ongoing struggle for religious freedom and cultural preservation:

Recognition of Tribal Sovereignty

The case affirmed the sovereignty of Native American tribes and their right to self-governance within their reservation bounds. It respected the authority of tribal courts to address crimes committed by tribal members on tribal land.

Protection of Religious Practices

The case underscored the importance of protecting indigenous religious practices, like the

Ghost Dance, as expressions of cultural and spiritual identity. It highlighted the need to respect and preserve these traditions in the face of government interference.

Legal Precedent

The Supreme Court's ruling in Crow Dog's Case set a legal precedent that would influence following decisions related to tribal jurisdiction and sovereignty. It contributed to the evolving body of law surrounding Native American rights.

Continued Struggle

While the case represented a significant victory for tribal sovereignty, Native American communities continued to face challenges in asserting their rights and preserving their cultural heritage. The struggle for land, resources, and the recognition of treaty rights persisted.

In conclusion, Crow Dog's Case stands as a landmark in the legal history of Native American rights and tribal sovereignty. It brought attention to the complex issues surrounding jurisdiction, the protection of religious practices, and the lasting struggle of indigenous communities to maintain their cultural identity in the face of profound challenges. The case remains a symbol of resilience and the ongoing quest for justice within Native American communities.

XXIII: ORENDA

Orenda, an Iroquoian term meaning "spiritual force," is a foundational concept in the belief system of the Iroquoian peoples, particularly the Haudenosaunee Confederacy, which includes the Mohawk, Oneida, Onondaga, Cayuga, Seneca, and later the Tuscarora nations. Orenda is a complex and multifaceted concept that includes the spiritual energy, power, and agency present in both human beings and the natural world. It plays a central place in shaping the worldview, culture, and social organization of the Iroquoian people, emphasizing the enmeshment of all living beings and the importance of maintaining harmony with the spiritual forces that permeate the universe.

Spiritual Energy and Necessary Force

At its core, orenda stands for the spiritual energy and necessary force that flows through all living entities, including human beings, animals, plants, and natural elements. It is the animating power that gives life and agency to all things. According to Iroquoian belief, every individual possesses their own unique orenda, which is a source of personal strength, wisdom, and agency. Orenda is not limited to humans; it exists in every aspect of the natural world, including animals, rocks, rivers, and celestial bodies.

Enmeshment and Balance

The concept of orenda underscores the profound enmeshment of all living beings and the environment. Iroquoian people view themselves as an integral part of the nexus of life, where everything is interconnected and interdependent. This enmeshment necessitates maintaining balance and harmony in all aspects of life. Disruptions to this balance, whether through human actions or natural occurrences, are believed to result from disturbances in the orenda.

Individual and Collective Orenda

In Iroquoian belief, individuals are responsible for nurturing and maintaining their personal orenda. This involves living in accordance with cultural and ethical values, making responsible choices, and participating in community life. The wellness of the individual is intimately tied to the wellness of the community, as the collective orenda is strengthened when individuals work together harmoniously.

Ceremonies and Rituals

Ceremonies and rituals hold a significant place in Iroquoian culture as means of harnessing and channeling orenda. Various rituals, like the Longhouse ceremonies, the Midwinter Ceremony, and the Green Corn Festival, are conducted to connect with spiritual forces, seek guidance, and express gratitude for the blessings of life. These ceremonies involve songs, dances, feasting, and offerings to honor the natural world and maintain balance.

Ethical Scaffolding

Orenda provides the ethical foundation for Iroquoian societies. It guides individuals in making moral decisions that are in alignment with the greater good of the community and the natural world. Acting in harmony with orenda means being respectful of all life forms, valuing cooperation and consensus, and seeking peace and balance in all aspects of life.

Healing and Medicine

Orenda is closely associated with traditional healing practices among the Iroquoian people. Healers and medicine people draw upon their own orenda and the collective orenda of the community to facilitate healing. Traditional remedies, ceremonies, and herbal medicine are employed to restore balance and wellness to individuals who are spiritually or physically ailing.

Relationship with the Natural World

The Iroquoian peoples maintain a profound connection with the natural world through orenda. They view the land, animals, and plants as spiritual beings with their own orenda. This perspective engenders a deep respect for the environment and an awareness of the consequences of humanity's actions on the balance of nature.

Leadership and Governance

The concept of orenda also extends to leadership and governance within Iroquoian societies. Leaders, known as chiefs, are chosen based on their demonstrated wisdom, integrity, and ability to embody the principles of orenda. Their leadership is seen as a responsibility to maintain the harmony and balance of the community and to uphold the collective orenda.

Adaptation and Resilience

Throughout history, Iroquoian peoples have faced significant challenges, including colonization, displacement, and cultural disruption. The concept of orenda has played an important place in their resilience and ability to adapt to changing circumstances. It has helped them maintain their cultural identity and traditions while navigating the complexities of the modern world.

Contemporary Relevance

Orenda remains a necessary and relevant concept in the lives of contemporary Iroquoian people. It continues to guide their actions, values, and relationships with the natural world. The teachings of orenda are passed down through generations, ensuring that the cultural and spiritual heritage of the Iroquoian nations endures.

Orenda is a profound and multifaceted concept that lies at the heart of the belief system of the Iroquoian peoples. It includes the spiritual energy, enmeshment, and balance that characterize their worldview. Orenda guides individual and collective actions, underpins ethical values, and encourages a deep respect for the natural world. It is a confirmation of the lasting wisdom and cultural resilience of the Iroquoian nations, who continue to draw strength from their spiritual heritage in their adventure through history and into the future.

XXIV: SKY WOMAN MYTHOLOGY

The Sky Woman Mythology is a central and foundational creation story within the religious and cultural traditions of the Iroquois Confederacy, also known as the Haudenosaunee. This complex and spiritually opulent narrative explains the origins of the world, the birth of humanity, and the enmeshment between the physical and spiritual worlds. The Sky Woman Mythology is not just a creation story but also a profound reflection of the Iroquois worldview, emphasizing themes of harmony, balance, and the essential place of women in the creation and sustenance of life.

The Creation of the World

The Sky Woman Myth begins with the existence of a celestial world inhabited by divine beings. In this upper world, there is a beautiful and radiant woman known as Sky Woman or Atahensic. Sky Woman is pregnant with twins, and her presence is a source of great light and warmth.

One day, Sky Woman becomes curious and peers deep into the celestial abyss. As she gazes into this darkness, she loses her balance and falls through a hole in the sky, plummeting towards the Earth below. Her fall is a momentous event, signifying the separation of the celestial world from the earthly world.

The Emergence of the Earth

As Sky Woman descends, animals and birds in the lower world notice her fall and gather together, recognizing the significance of her arrival. They discuss the need for a solid place for her to land, and the creatures work together to create a space for her. Various animals take turns diving to the ocean floor to bring back mud to form the Earth.

The creatures continue their efforts, and with the combined contributions of animals and birds, they gradually build a stable landmass. Sky Woman safely lands on this newly formed Earth, where she gives birth to her twin sons, Sapling and Flint. These twin sons hold a necessary place in the following creation of humanity and the natural world.

The Birth of Humanity

As Sky Woman's sons, Sapling and Flint, grow, they begin to shape the world around them. Sapling takes on the place of the creator of life, fashioning animals and plants from the mud and clay of the Earth. He breathes life into these beings, and they come to life, filling the land, waters, and skies. Flint, on the other hand, is responsible for shaping the territory and providing essential resources for the newly created beings. He forms mountains, lakes, and rivers, and he ensures the availability of stones and minerals. Together, Sapling and Flint collaborate to bring balance and harmony to the world they are shaping. They embody the dual forces of creation and preservation, emphasizing the need for equilibrium and enmeshment in the natural world.

The Place of Women in Creation

The Sky Woman Mythology places a significant emphasis on the place of women in the creation of life and the preservation of cultural values. Sky Woman herself is a symbol of the maternal and life-giving aspects of creation, as she is the mother of humanity. Women in Iroquois society are revered for their wisdom, strength, and nurturing qualities, reflecting the importance of female leadership and guidance. In the Iroquois Confederacy, women hold a central position within the clan structure, with clans being matrilineal and descent being traced through the mother's line. Women are responsible for maintaining the spiritual and cultural traditions of the community, passing down knowledge, and ensuring the wellness of future generations.

The Importance of Balance and Harmony

The Sky Woman Mythology highlights the fundamental principles of balance and harmony that underlie the Iroquois worldview. The collaboration between the twin sons, Sapling and Flint, stands for the complementary forces of creation and preservation. This duality is mirrored in the natural world, where cycles of life, death, and renewal are interconnected and essential for maintaining equilibrium. The story also focuses on the enmeshment of all living beings, highlighting the need for respect and stewardship of the Earth and its resources. It underscores the Iroquois belief that humans are not separate from nature but are integral parts of the nexus of life.

Spiritual Significance

The Sky Woman Mythology is not merely a historical narrative; it holds profound spiritual significance for the Iroquois people. It provides a scaffolding for understanding the enmeshment of all life, the importance of balance, and the place of women in the preservation of cultural values. The narrative is often invoked in ceremonies, rituals, and storytelling within Iroquois communities. It acts as a source of guidance, encouragement, and cultural identity, reminding the people of their spiritual responsibilities to the Earth and each other.

Contemporary Relevance

The Sky Woman Mythology remains a living and relevant part of the cultural and spiritual heritage of the Iroquois Confederacy. It continues to shape the worldview and values of Iroquois communities, encouraging a deep connection to the land and a commitment to preserving cultural traditions.

In conclusion, the Sky Woman Mythology is a profound creation story within the Iroquois religious and cultural traditions. It not just explains the origins of the world and humanity but also conveys essential teachings about balance, harmony, and the enmeshment of all life. This narrative highlights the necessary place of women in the creation and preservation of cultural values, reflecting the Iroquois belief in the importance of female leadership and wisdom. The story's lasting spiritual significance underscores its continued relevance in contemporary Iroquois communities, where it guides and inspires future generations.

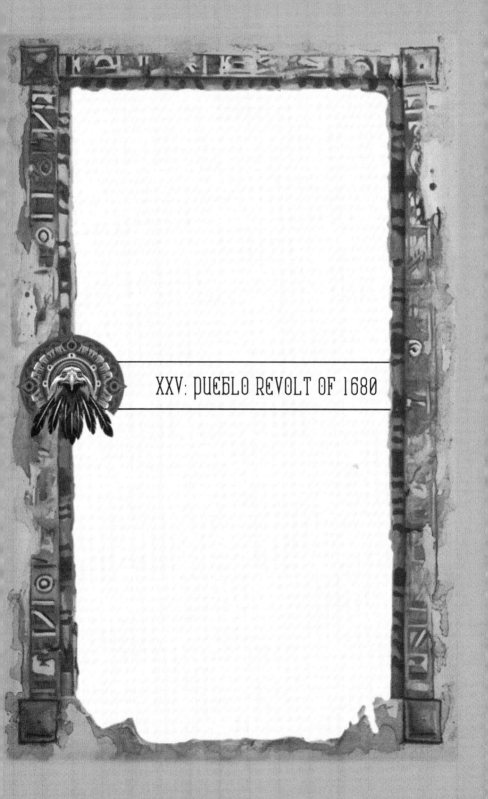

XXV: PUEBLO REVOLT OF 1680

The Pueblo Revolt of 1680, also known as Pope's Rebellion, is a necessary event in the history of Spanish colonization of the American Southwest. This rebellion was deeply founded in the religious beliefs and practices of the Pueblo people, who inhabited the region that is now New Mexico and Arizona. The revolt marked a significant chapter in the complex and often tumultuous interactions between Indigenous peoples and European colonizers in North America. It demonstrated the resilience of Indigenous cultures and the determination to preserve their traditions, including their spiritual and religious practices.

Spanish Colonization in the American Southwest
The Spanish colonization of the American Southwest began in earnest in the late 16th century, with the establishment of settlements, missions, and military outposts in the region. The Spanish searched out to expand their territorial claims and convert Indigenous populations to Christianity. Franciscan missionaries played a central place in these efforts, aiming to convert the Pueblo people to Roman Catholicism and assimilate them into Spanish colonial society. The arrival of the Spanish brought significant changes to the Pueblo way of life. The Pueblo people were subjected to forced labor, known as the encomienda system, and faced exploitation and cultural suppression. They were expected to adopt Spanish customs, including the

Christian faith, and were subjected to harsh treatment by Spanish authorities and missionaries.

Effect on Pueblo Religion and Culture

The introduction of Christianity and the suppression of traditional Pueblo religious practices had a profound effect on Pueblo society. The Pueblo people faced cultural disruption and the erosion of their traditional belief systems, which were deeply intertwined with their relationship with the land, nature, and the spiritual world. Pueblo religion was polytheistic, emphasizing the veneration of deities associated with natural elements, seasonal cycles, and agricultural fertility. As the Spanish imposed their religious and cultural practices, Pueblo religious ceremonies and rituals were banned, sacred kivas (ceremonial chambers) were destroyed or repurposed, and traditional religious leaders were persecuted. The Pueblo people found themselves torn between preserving their ancestral beliefs and adapting to the pressures of Spanish colonization.

Religious Suppression and Resistance

Despite the efforts of Spanish authorities and missionaries to suppress Pueblo religious practices, many Pueblo individuals and communities secretly continued to observe their traditional ceremonies and rituals. These acts of resistance were carried out in the secrecy of kivas and remote locations to avoid detection. Pueblo religious leaders, known as shamans or religious practitioners, played an important place in preserving their people's spiritual traditions. They provided spiritual guidance, performed ceremonies, and maintained a connection to the deities and ancestral spirits. The suppression of their place and practices only fueled the desire to resist Spanish influence and reclaim their cultural and religious autonomy.

The Place of Pope

Pope, also known as Po'pay or Popé, emerged as a prominent and charismatic religious leader among the Pueblo people. He was a medicine man from the Tewa-speaking village of Ohkay Owingeh (formerly San Juan Pueblo). Pope was deeply committed to preserving Pueblo religious traditions and opposing Spanish colonization. Pope was instrumental in uniting various Pueblo villages and communities in a coordinated effort to resist Spanish rule. He organized a ever-present and carefully coordinated uprising that would become the Pueblo Revolt of 1680. His leadership was grounded in his spiritual authority and his vision of a Pueblo world free from Spanish domination.

The Pueblo Revolt of 1680

On August 10, 1680, the Pueblo Revolt erupted across the Spanish-controlled settlements in present-day New Mexico. Coordinated by Pope, Pueblo warriors and religious leaders rose up against the Spanish colonizers. The revolt was not just a political and military uprising but also a profound religious and cultural movement aimed at restoring traditional Pueblo ways of life and spirituality. The Pueblo warriors, armed with traditional weapons and a deep sense of purpose, attacked Spanish settlements and missions, driving the colonizers out of the region. The Spanish were forced to retreat to the south, and for several years, the Pueblo people regained control over their ancestral lands.

Reestablishment of Traditional Practices

With the Spanish gone, the Pueblo people began on a process of cultural and religious renewal. They rebuilt their kivas, revived traditional ceremonies, and reinstated their religious leaders. The Pueblo Revolt was not just a successful political and military resistance but also a spiritual and cultural awakening, with Pueblo religious practices at its core. The reestablishment of traditional practices was an act of cultural resilience and a confirmation of the lasting power of Pueblo spirituality. The Pueblo people searched out to reconnect with their ancestral deities and reaffirm their spiritual connection to the land.

Aftermath and Spanish Return

The Pueblo Revolt of 1680 led to a period of relative independence for the Pueblo communities in the American Southwest. However, the Spanish were determined to regain control of the region. In 1692, under the leadership of Diego de Vargas, the Spanish launched a campaign to reconquer New Mexico. This period, known as the Reconquest, resulted in the reestablishment of Spanish rule in many Pueblo villages. The Spanish, recognizing the deep ties between the Pueblo religion and their cultural identity, adopted a more lenient approach toward Pueblo religious practices. While they continued to promote Christianity, they allowed the Pueblo people greater freedom in practicing their traditional ceremonies and rituals. This policy of accommodation marked a departure from the earlier era of religious suppression.

Heritage and Significance

The Pueblo Revolt of 1680 holds immense significance in American history. It stands as one of the most successful and sustained Indigenous uprisings against European colonization in North America. The revolt showcased the resilience of Pueblo culture and religion in the face of external pressures and the determination of Indigenous people to protect their way of life. The events of 1680 left a lasting effect on the Pueblo communities and their relationship with the Spanish and later Mexican and American authorities. The Pueblo people managed to maintain a degree of cultural and religious autonomy, allowing their traditional spirituality to coexist with external influences.

The Pueblo Revolt of 1680 was a remarkable historical event deeply founded in Pueblo religious beliefs and the determination to preserve cultural and spiritual traditions. It marked a necessary moment in the history of Spanish colonization in the American Southwest and remains a confirmation of the lasting power of Indigenous spirituality and cultural resilience. The revolt acts as a reminder of the complexities and lasting legacies of colonization and the ongoing efforts of Indigenous peoples to protect and revitalize their traditions.

XXVI: cannupa

The Cannupa, known as the "sacred pipe" in Lakota and other Plains tribes, holds profound spiritual significance in Indigenous cultures of the Great Plains of North America. This sacred object is central to various rituals, ceremonies, and religious practices, serving as a symbol of unity, prayer, and connection to the spiritual world. The significance of the Cannupa extends beyond its physical form; it embodies the core values, beliefs, and cosmology of the Plains tribes, particularly the Lakota Sioux, and plays a necessary place in their relationship with the Creator, the land, and all living beings.

The Sacred Pipe as a Gift from the Creator

In Lakota and Plains tribal traditions, the sacred pipe is believed to be a gift from the Creator, Wakan Tanka, who is the ultimate source of life, wisdom, and spiritual guidance. The pipe is respected as a physical manifestation of the Creator's presence and a means of communication between the human and spiritual worlds. It is often referred to as "The Chante Ishta," which translates to "the pipe of prayer." According to oral traditions, the sacred pipe was brought to the Lakota people by the White Buffalo Calf Woman (Ptesáŋwiŋ Wiŋ) or other divine messengers, depending on the tribal variation of the story. The White Buffalo Calf Woman is a revered figure in Lakota mythology and is believed to have provided the Lakota with the sacred pipe and teachings on how to use it in ceremonies.

The Pipe's Components and Symbolism

The Cannupa consists of several essential components, each of which carries its own symbolism and significance:

Bowl (Bowl of the Pipe)

The bowl is typically made of a specific type of red pipestone, known as catlinite, and stands for the earth. It symbolizes the physical world and the connection to the land, plants, and animals.

Stem (Stem of the Pipe)

The stem stands for the human connection to the spiritual world. It symbolizes the breath of life and the bridge between the earthly and spiritual dimensions. The stem is often made from wood, like ash or cedar.

Feathers

Feathers are often attached to the stem of the sacred pipe, representing the connection between humans and the winged beings, like birds, which are respected as messengers and carriers of prayers to the Creator.

Tobacco

The tobacco used in the sacred pipe is specifically cultivated and prepared for ceremonial use. It stands for the breath of life, prayer, and the offering of thanks to the Creator. Tobacco is respected as a sacred plant with spiritual properties.

Pipe Bag

The pipe is typically kept in a specially crafted pipe bag made of leather or other materials. The pipe bag protects the sacred object and is adorned with various symbols and designs, reflecting the owner's spiritual adventure and affiliations.

The Ritual and Ceremonial Use of the Sacred Pipe

The sacred pipe is used in various ceremonies and rituals within Plains tribes, with the most well-known being the Pipe Ceremony. The Pipe Ceremony is a sacred and solemn occasion that involves prayers, offerings, and the sharing of the pipe among participants. It is a way to connect with the Creator, express gratitude, seek guidance, and pray for the wellness of individuals, the community, and the world. During the Pipe Ceremony, the pipe is filled with tobacco, and prayers are offered to the four cardinal directions, representing the enmeshment of all living beings and the spiritual significance of the natural world. Participants take turns smoking the pipe and passing it to one another, symbolizing unity, community, and the sharing of blessings. The smoke from the pipe is believed to carry the prayers and intentions of the participants to the Creator. The sacred pipe is also used in other ceremonies, like sweat lodge ceremonies, vision quests, and healing rituals. It acts as a tool for spiritual purification, guidance, and communion with the spiritual world.

The Significance of the Cannupa in Plains Tribal Life
The Cannupa is not limited to ceremonial use but is integrated into various aspects of Plains tribal life. It holds a central place in tribal governance and decision-making processes, with tribal leaders often using the sacred pipe during council meetings to seek guidance from the Creator and make important decisions for the community. Additionally, the pipe is an essential component of rites of passage, like coming-of-age ceremonies and weddings, symbolizing the sacredness of these life transitions. It is also used in times of crisis or hardship, serving as a source of strength, comfort, and resilience for individuals and communities facing challenges. The significance of the sacred pipe extends to the broader cultural identity of Plains tribes. It embodies the values of humility, respect, and enmeshment, which are central to their worldview. The pipe reinforces the importance of maintaining a harmonious relationship with the land, the natural world, and all living beings.

The Contemporary Place of the Sacred Pipe
Today, the sacred pipe continues to hold a necessary place in the spiritual and cultural life of

197

Plains tribes. While Native communities have faced numerous challenges, including colonization, forced assimilation, and cultural disruption, the sacred pipe remains a symbol of resilience and cultural preservation. Efforts to protect and revitalize the traditions associated with the sacred pipe are ongoing, with many Indigenous individuals and organizations working to ensure that these practices are passed down to future generations. The sacred pipe acts as a source of strength, identity, and spiritual connection for Native communities, reinforcing the lasting importance of their cultural heritage.

The Cannupa, or sacred pipe, is a central and sacred element of Lakota and Plains tribal spirituality and culture. It stands for the profound connection between the physical and spiritual worlds, the relationship between humans and the Creator, and the unity of all living beings. The significance of the sacred pipe extends beyond its physical form, encompassing the values, beliefs, and cosmology of Plains tribes. It acts as a symbol of resilience, cultural preservation, and the lasting spiritual strength of Indigenous communities in the face of historical challenges.

XXVII: navajo skinwalkers

The Navajo skinwalkers, known as "Yee Naaldlooshii" in the Navajo language, are enigmatic and feared beings deeply entrenched in Navajo lore and cultural beliefs. These shape-shifting entities occupy a complex and mystical world within Navajo cosmology, carrying with them a sense of taboo and dread. The legend of the skinwalkers remains one of the most interesting and enigmatic aspects of Navajo spirituality, drawing both fascination and caution from those who encounter their stories.

Origins and Nature of Skinwalkers
In Navajo belief, the skinwalkers are believed to be practitioners of a dark and malevolent form of witchcraft, referred to as "witchery" or "yee naaldlooshii." These individuals, often seen as rogue or renegade medicine people or shamans, have chosen to use their knowledge and power for malevolent purposes. It is said that they possess the ability to transform into animals or other people, allowing them to carry out their harmful deeds while concealing their true identities. The term "skinwalker" itself refers to their ability to wear the skin of animals, effectively adopting their physical forms. This transformation is not seen as an innate power but rather the result of a deeply unnatural and sinister act, often involving the use of dark rituals and supernatural knowledge.

The Dark Side of Transformation

The transformation ability of skinwalkers is not viewed within Navajo culture as a gift or a form of spiritual growth but rather as a grave transgression against the natural order and the sacredness of life. It is respected as an act of extreme taboo to engage in such practices, as it involves the deliberate violation of cultural and spiritual norms. The skinwalker's ability to change form is seen as an inversion of the traditional Navajo belief in transformation, which is typically associated with positive and healing practices. In contrast, the skinwalker's transformation is an expression of malevolence and a departure from the harmony and balance central to Navajo spirituality.

Malevolence and Harmful Deeds

Skinwalkers are believed to use their shape-shifting abilities for a variety of harmful purposes. They may employ their powers to cause illness, injury, or death to individuals, often as part of personal vendettas or for material gain. Some legends suggest that they have the ability to steal the life force or essence of their victims. These malevolent actions are not just directed at humans but also extend to livestock, often resulting in unexplained deaths or ailments among animals. This has led to a deep fear and suspicion surrounding the presence of skinwalkers in Navajo communities.

The Place of Fear and Secrecy

The legend of the skinwalkers instills a profound sense of fear and caution within Navajo culture. The belief in their existence is ever-present, and the consequences of encountering or identifying a skinwalker can be dire. Navajo people are often hesitant to openly discuss or share information about skinwalkers due to the fear of retaliation or the potential harm they may bring. Furthermore, the taboo surrounding skinwalkers has led to a reluctance to dive into the details of their practices or to adventure through their origins and motivations. The fear of inadvertently invoking or attracting the attention of these malevolent beings reinforces the importance of maintaining secrecy.

Protection and Safeguards

Navajo individuals and communities take various precautions to protect themselves from the perceived threat of skinwalkers. These precautions may include the use of protective amulets, blessings, and ceremonies performed by traditional healers or medicine people. Certain herbs and rituals are believed to deter or ward off the presence of skinwalkers. Traditional Navajo ceremonies, like the Blessingway or the Enemyway, are often conducted to restore harmony and balance in cases where the influence of a skinwalker is suspected. These ceremonies serve as a means of healing and protection, reaffirming the importance of cultural practices and spiritual wellness.

The Complexity of Identity
Identifying a skinwalker is often challenging within Navajo culture due to their ability to conceal their true identities. Suspicion may fall on individuals who exhibit unusual behaviors or possess a reputation for malevolent actions. However, making definitive accusations is fraught with risk, as it can provoke retaliation or harm. The notion of skinwalkers raises questions about the bounds of identity and the thin line between individuals who use their knowledge for healing and those who choose to employ it for harm. This duality underscores the complexity of Navajo spirituality and the place of individual choices within a cultural and spiritual scaffolding.

Contemporary Perspectives
In modern times, the legend of the skinwalkers continues to be a topic of fascination and intrigue, both within and beyond Navajo culture. Stories and accounts of encounters with alleged skinwalkers are shared among individuals, contributing to the lasting mystique of these beings. However, it is important to recognize that the belief in skinwalkers remains deeply founded in Navajo cultural and spiritual traditions. It is not a subject to be taken lightly or sensationalized. For many Navajo

people, the fear and respect associated with skinwalkers are a reminder of the importance of maintaining cultural values, respecting the natural order, and living in harmony with the spiritual world.

In conclusion, the Navajo skinwalkers, or Yee Naaldlooshii, are beings of immense fear and mystery in Navajo culture. Their shape-shifting abilities, malevolent actions, and violation of cultural norms make them a subject of both caution and fascination. The legend of the skinwalkers is a reminder of the profound importance of cultural values, spiritual harmony, and the lasting belief systems that shape the worldview of the Navajo people.

XXVIII: TURTLE ISLAND

Turtle Island is a powerful and recurring motif in the creation stories and cosmologies of many Indigenous North American tribes. This symbol stands for the Earth itself and holds deep spiritual and cultural significance. The concept of Turtle Island transcends individual tribal bounds, uniting Indigenous peoples across the continent in their shared understanding of the Earth's origins and their place within the natural world. This narrative theme, charted into the atlas of Indigenous knowledge, reflects the enmeshment of all life, the importance of stewardship, and the lasting relationship between Indigenous peoples and their homelands.

The Origin of Turtle Island

The story of Turtle Island varies among different Indigenous tribes, reflecting the opulent diversity of cultures across North America. While there are variations in the details of the creation narrative, the overarching theme centers on the emergence of the Earth from the waters, often symbolized by the back of a giant turtle.

In the Ojibwe creation story, the Earth is referred to as "Turtle Island" because it is said to have formed on the back of a great turtle. According to Ojibwe tradition, this turtle emerged from the primordial waters of the Great Sea and provided a foundation for the Earth. The continents, mountains, and landscapes we see today are seen as the result of the turtle's emergence and transformation.

Among the Haudenosaunee (Iroquois) Confederacy, which includes the Mohawk, Oneida, Onondaga, Cayuga, Seneca, and Tuscarora nations, there is a similar narrative. In their creation story, it is the Sky Woman who descends from the upper world and lands on the back of a giant turtle. With the help of various animals, she forms the Earth from the soil collected from the ocean floor, giving rise to Turtle Island.

These narratives highlight the profound connection between Indigenous peoples and their homelands, reinforcing the idea that the Earth is a living being, and humans are its caretakers.

Sacred Symbolism of the Turtle

The turtle itself carries deep spiritual symbolism in Indigenous cultures. It is often associated with longevity, wisdom, patience, and resilience. Its slow and deliberate movements reflect an understanding of the importance of taking one's time and making deliberate choices. The turtle's shell is seen as a protective barrier, representing safety and strength. These qualities are not just embodied by the turtle but are also ascribed to Turtle Island, the Earth itself.

In some Indigenous traditions, the shell of the turtle is divided into thirteen segments, corresponding to the thirteen lunar cycles in a year.

The turtle's back thus becomes a lunar calendar, linking the cycles of nature to the passage of time. This sacred symbolism underscores the Indigenous understanding of the Earth's rhythms and the importance of living in harmony with them.

The Spiritual and Cultural Significance

Turtle Island is not merely a creation story; it is a foundational element of Indigenous spirituality and cultural identity. It provides a scaffolding for understanding the relationship between humans and the Earth and the responsibilities that come with living on Turtle Island. Indigenous peoples view themselves as caretakers of the land, entrusted with the duty of preserving its integrity and maintaining balance within the natural world. The concept of Turtle Island focuses on the idea that the Earth is a living entity deserving of respect, protection, and stewardship.

Furthermore, Turtle Island acts as a reminder of the enmeshment of all life. In Indigenous cosmologies, humans are respected as one part of a giant nexus of existence, with plants, animals, waters, and celestial bodies all holding integral roles in the complex atlas of creation. This interconnected worldview encourages reverence for all living beings and a commitment to living in harmony with the Earth's rhythms.

Contemporary Relevance

The concept of Turtle Island remains highly relevant in contemporary Indigenous thought and activism. Indigenous peoples continue to advocate for the protection of their homelands, the preservation of traditional ecological knowledge, and the recognition of their rights as stewards of the Earth. Efforts to address environmental challenges, like climate change, land degradation, and habitat loss, are informed by Indigenous perspectives on the sacredness of Turtle Island. Indigenous communities across North America are at the forefront of environmental conservation initiatives, emphasizing the need to respect the Earth's careful balance and heal the wounds inflicted upon it. Turtle Island is also a unifying symbol for Indigenous peoples, transcending tribal bounds. It encourages a sense of shared identity and purpose among diverse Indigenous nations, providing a common ground for collective action and cultural revitalization.

Cultural Expressions and Artifacts

The symbolism of Turtle Island is mirrored in various forms of Indigenous art and cultural expressions. It can be found in the complex beadwork, pottery, and basketry of Native artists, as well as in traditional songs and dances that celebrate the Earth's bounty. Turtle Island is a source of encouragement for contemporary Indigenous artists, who use their creativity to convey the lasting connection between their cultures and the land. Additionally, turtle effigies and sculptures are common in Indigenous artwork and can be found in museums and galleries across North America. These pieces serve as reminders of the cultural and spiritual significance of the turtle and Turtle Island.

Turtle Island, with its opulent atlas of creation stories and spiritual symbolism, stands as a confirmation of the profound connection between Indigenous peoples and the Earth. It embodies the Indigenous worldview, emphasizing the importance of stewardship, reverence for all life, and the enmeshment of existence. The concept of Turtle Island is not confined to the past; it remains a living and dynamic expression of Indigenous spirituality and cultural identity. It informs contemporary efforts to protect the environment, revitalize traditional knowledge, and promote Indigenous rights and sovereignty. Turtle Island acts as a bridge between Indigenous traditions and the broader world, offering a perspective founded in respect for the Earth and its diverse inhabitants. It invites all people to reflect on their relationship with the natural world and to recognize the enmeshment of all life on this shared home, Turtle Island.

XXIX: SWEAT LODGES

Sweat lodge ceremonies hold a profound and sacred place in the spiritual practices of many Indigenous cultures across North America. These ceremonies are marked by their intense heat, profound symbolism, and deep spiritual significance. Sweatlodge songs and prayers are integral components of these ceremonies, holding a necessary place in guiding participants through the experience, connecting them with the spiritual world, and reinforcing the sacredness of the ritual. The specific songs and prayers used in sweat lodge ceremonies vary among different Indigenous tribes and communities, reflecting the diversity of their cultural traditions and beliefs.

The Significance of Sweat Lodge Ceremonies

Sweat lodge ceremonies, also known as "inipi" among the Lakota Sioux and by various other names in different Indigenous languages, are conducted within a small, dome-shaped structure typically made of wooden or willow branches and covered with blankets or hides. Heated stones, often referred to as "grandfathers" or "hot rocks," are placed in a central pit within the lodge. Water infused with medicinal herbs, like sage or cedar, is poured over these rocks, creating steam and intense heat. Participants sit in a circle, symbolizing the sacred hoop of life. The sweat lodge stands for the womb of Mother Earth, and the ceremony itself symbolizes a adventure of purification, rebirth, and spiritual renewal. The experience within the sweat lodge is both physically and spiritually demanding, with the extreme heat serving as a means of cleansing the body and spirit. Participants engage in prayer, song, and reflection, seeking guidance, healing, and a deeper connection to the Creator and the natural world.

The Place of Songs and Prayers

Songs and prayers are at the heart of the sweat lodge ceremony, guiding participants through the various stages of the ritual and providing a spiritual foundation for the experience. These songs and prayers are typically led by a designated spiritual leader, often referred to as a "firekeeper" or "lodge leader." The songs are typically sung in the native language of the tribe, contributing to the ceremony's authenticity and cultural continuity.

Purification and Healing Prayers

Purification and healing are central themes in sweat lodge ceremonies. Participants enter the lodge with specific intentions, seeking physical, emotional, or spiritual healing. The prayers uttered within the sweat lodge often focus on these intentions, calling upon the Creator, the spirits, and the natural world to provide guidance and support in the adventure towards wholeness. The firekeeper or lodge leader may offer purification prayers that acknowledge the sacredness of the lodge and its connection to the natural elements, like fire, water, earth, and air. These prayers help set the tone for the ceremony and reinforce the significance of the experience.

Connecting with Ancestors and Spirits

Sweat lodge ceremonies provide a unique opportunity for participants to connect with their ancestors and the spiritual world. Songs and prayers often invoke the presence of these ancestors, calling upon their wisdom, guidance, and protection. The lodge is seen as a portal to the spirit world, where communication with ancestors and spirits is facilitated. The songs and prayers used in this context serve as a bridge between the physical and spiritual worlds, facilitating communication and communion with the unseen forces that shape the world. Participants may experience visions, receive messages, or feel a profound sense of spiritual connection during the ceremony.

Songs of Gratitude and Blessings

Expressing gratitude and seeking blessings are common themes in sweat lodge songs and prayers. Participants often offer prayers of thanksgiving for the gifts of life, the Earth, and the Creator. These expressions of gratitude acknowledge the enmeshment of all life and the importance of living in harmony with the natural world. Blessing songs are also sung to invoke divine blessings and protection. These songs call upon the Creator and the spirits to watch over and guide the participants, ensuring their safety and wellness throughout the ceremony and beyond.

Cultural Diversity in Sweat Lodge Ceremonies
It is important to note that the specific songs and prayers used in sweat lodge ceremonies vary widely among Indigenous tribes and communities. Each tribe has its own unique traditions, languages, and ceremonial practices, which are passed down through generations. For example, among the Lakota Sioux, the inipi ceremony is a central component of their spiritual traditions, and specific songs and prayers are associated with it. Similarly, other tribes, like the Ojibwe, Navajo, Apache, and many more, have their own variations of sweat lodge ceremonies, each with its distinct songs, prayers, and rituals. These cultural variations reflect the diversity and richness of Indigenous spiritual practices and highlight the importance of respecting and preserving the unique traditions of each tribe.

The Contemporary Relevance of Sweat Lodge Ceremonies
Sweat lodge ceremonies continue to be a necessary and living part of Indigenous spirituality and cultural identity in the contemporary world. Despite historical challenges, including colonization and forced assimilation, Indigenous communities have persevered in maintaining their sacred

traditions. Today, sweat lodge ceremonies are experiencing a resurgence among Indigenous peoples as a means of cultural revitalization and spiritual healing. These ceremonies hold a necessary place in addressing the historical trauma and social challenges that many Indigenous communities face.

Additionally, non-Indigenous individuals and communities have shown interest in participating in sweat lodge ceremonies as a means of cultural exchange and spiritual adventure. It is essential that such participation is done with the utmost respect for Indigenous traditions, with permission and guidance from Indigenous spiritual leaders, and with a deep understanding of the cultural and spiritual significance of the ceremony.

Sweat lodge ceremonies are deeply founded in the spiritual and cultural traditions of Indigenous North American tribes. Songs and prayers are the heartbeat of these ceremonies, guiding participants through purification, healing, and spiritual communion. These ceremonies remain a source of strength, resilience, and cultural continuity for Indigenous communities, emphasizing the importance of maintaining a harmonious relationship with the natural world and seeking spiritual guidance from the Creator and the spirits. Sweat lodge ceremonies continue to be a necessary and evolving aspect of Indigenous spirituality in the contemporary world.

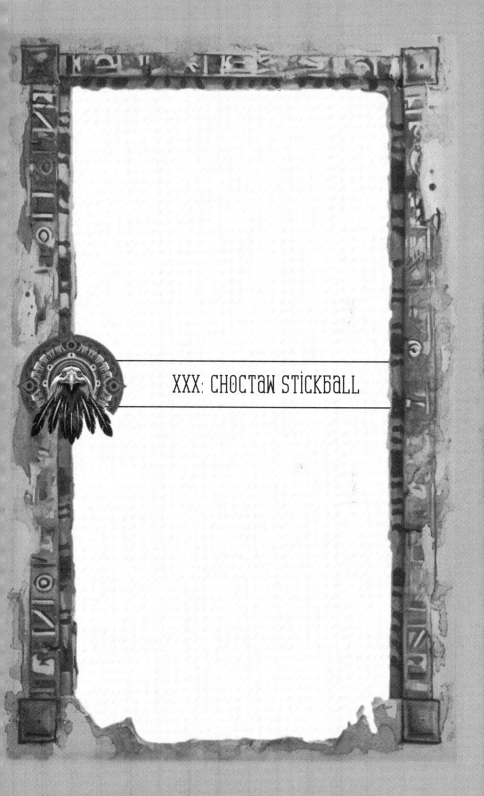

XXX: CHOCTAW STICKBALL

Choctaw Stickball, often referred to as "the little brother of war," is a traditional Indigenous game with deep spiritual, cultural, and historical significance among the Choctaw Nation and other Southeastern tribes. This ancient game is much more than a sport; it is a reflection of Choctaw cosmology, spirituality, and a means of preserving tribal identity. The game's origins date back centuries, and it continues to be an essential part of Choctaw cultural practices, serving as a way to connect with ancestors, express tribal values, and encourage community bonds.

Historical and Cultural Significance

Choctaw Stickball, or "Lacrosse" as it is commonly known among Native American communities, has an opulent history that predates European contact. It was not merely a form of entertainment but served as a way for Choctaw warriors to hone their skills, encourage unity, and prepare for battle. The game was often played to settle disputes, celebrate victories, or offer gratitude to the Creator for bountiful harvests. The game's spiritual significance is evident in its connection to Choctaw cosmology. The two sticks used in Stickball represent the duality of life, symbolizing the balance between light and darkness, good and evil, and harmony and conflict. The sticks are carved with complex designs, each carrying specific spiritual meanings.

Gameplay and Rituals

Choctaw Stickball is played on a field that can be several hundred yards long. Two teams, each consisting of multiple players, compete to score goals by hitting a ball, traditionally made of deerskin or a wooden ball covered in hide, through the opponent's goalpost using stickball sticks. Before the game begins, various rituals and ceremonies take place, often overseen by a spiritual leader or medicine person. These rituals serve to bless the players, the sticks, and the field, ensuring that the game is conducted in a manner that respects the Creator and honors the traditions of the Choctaw Nation. One of the most notable aspects of Stickball is the use of traditional Choctaw songs and dances throughout the game. Drummers and singers accompany the players, providing a rhythmic and spiritual backdrop to the action on the field. These songs and dances carry deep cultural and spiritual significance, invoking the spirits of ancestors and reinforcing the unity of the Choctaw people.

Spiritual Elements and Symbolism

Stickball is respected as a sacred game by the Choctaw people, and it is imbued with spiritual elements that go beyond the physical competition. The spiritual significance of Stickball is mirrored in several key aspects:

Connection to Ancestors

Stickball acts as a way to connect with the spirits of ancestors. Players often honor their forebears through the game, seeking their guidance and protection. The actions on the field are seen as a continuation of the heritage of Choctaw warriors and the preservation of tribal identity.

Harmony and Balance

The symbolism of the sticks and the duality they represent emphasize the importance of harmony and balance in life. Players are encouraged to maintain equilibrium in their actions, both on and off the field. Stickball is a reminder that life is a careful dance between opposing forces, and maintaining balance is essential.

Prayer and Gratitude

Choctaw Stickball is infused with prayer and expressions of gratitude to the Creator. Players acknowledge the blessings they have received and offer thanks for the opportunity to participate in the game. It is a way to connect with the spiritual world and show appreciation for the gifts of life.

Community Bonding

Stickball encourages a sense of community and unity among the Choctaw people. It brings individuals and families together, reinforcing the bonds that hold the tribe together. The game acts as a spiritual and cultural glue that helps preserve tribal identity.

Respect for Nature

The traditional materials used in Stickball, like deerskin and wooden sticks, reflect the Choctaw people's deep respect for nature. These materials are sustainably sourced, and their use underscores the tribe's harmonious relationship with the natural world.

Contemporary Significance

In contemporary times, Choctaw Stickball continues to hold immense cultural importance. The game is a source of pride and identity for the Choctaw Nation and other Southeastern tribes. Efforts are underway to preserve and revitalize this ancient tradition, ensuring that it is passed down to future generations.

Choctaw Stickball tournaments and events are held to show the game's cultural significance and promote its practice among tribal members. These events often feature traditional songs, dances, and ceremonies alongside the athletic competition, reinforcing the spiritual and cultural aspects of Stickball.

Choctaw Stickball, known as "the little brother of war," is far more than a sport; it is a spiritual and cultural cornerstone of the Choctaw Nation and other Southeastern tribes. This ancient game acts as a bridge between the past and the present, connecting Choctaw people with their ancestors, their traditions, and the Creator. The game's deep spiritual elements, symbolism, and rituals underscore the importance of balance, harmony, and unity within the Choctaw culture. In the face of modern challenges, Choctaw Stickball remains a powerful and resilient expression of Indigenous identity and spirituality.

XXXI: MEDICINE WHEEL

The Medicine Wheel, a symbol of profound spiritual significance, is a common element in the cosmologies and teachings of various Native American cultures across North America. This sacred circle stands for not just the enmeshment of all life but also acts as a guide for understanding the natural world, the self, and the Creator. While the specific interpretations and teachings of the Medicine Wheel vary among tribes, there are common themes and elements that underscore its universal spiritual significance.

The Circular Symbolism

At its core, the Medicine Wheel is a circle divided into four quadrants or directions: North, East, South, and West. The circular shape stands for the cyclical nature of life, the enmeshment of all things, and the continuous adventure of existence. The circle has no beginning or end, symbolizing the eternal and holistic nature of the universe.

The Four Directions

Each of the four directions within the Medicine Wheel holds specific teachings, symbolism, and associations:

North

The North is often associated with wisdom, introspection, and the season of winter. It stands for the elder years of life, where one gains insight and understanding through experience. The element of Earth is typically associated with the North, emphasizing stability and grounding.

East

The East signifies new beginnings, the rising sun, and the dawn of each day. It stands for the birth and growth of life and is associated with the element of Air, signifying breath and communication. The East teaches the importance of clarity, illumination, and renewal.

South

The South stands for the heat of summer, passion, and adolescence. It symbolizes growth, vitality, and the element of Fire. This direction teaches about the energy and determination required to achieve one's goals and desires.

West

The West is associated with the setting sun, evening, and the season of autumn. It signifies transformation, introspection, and the element of Water. The West teaches the lessons of letting go, adapting to change, and embracing the cycles of life.

The Center and the Creator

The center of the Medicine Wheel is often regarded as the point of balance and harmony. It stands for the here and now, the present moment, and the connection to the Creator or Great Spirit. The Creator is seen as the source of all life and the force that sustains the universe. The teachings of the center emphasize the importance of being present, seeking balance in all things, and acknowledging the divine presence within and around us.

The Sacred Number Four

The number four is a fundamental aspect of Medicine Wheel teachings. It reflects the four directions, the four seasons, the four elements (Earth, Air, Fire, and Water), and the four stages of life (birth, growth, maturity, and transformation). The repetition of this number underscores the idea of completeness and balance within the Medicine Wheel's teachings.

Personal and Collective Growth

The Medicine Wheel is a tool for both personal and collective growth. It provides a scaffolding for understanding the stages and cycles of life, offering guidance on how to navigate challenges and find meaning in each phase. It focuses on the enmeshment of individuals with their communities and the natural world, highlighting the responsibility to maintain harmony and balance in all relationships.

Rituals and Ceremonies

The Medicine Wheel is often incorporated into various Indigenous rituals and ceremonies. These ceremonies may include offerings, prayers, songs, and dances that align with the teachings of the Medicine Wheel. For example, the Wheel might be used in vision quests, healing ceremonies, or rites of passage to mark significant life transitions.

Cultural Diversity

While the core teachings of the Medicine Wheel are shared among many Native American cultures, there are also variations and unique interpretations based on tribal traditions and geographical locations. Different tribes may have specific symbols, colors, or rituals associated with their Medicine Wheel teachings. For example, the Lakota Sioux have their own version of the Medicine Wheel, which includes the color symbolism of red, yellow, black, and white.

Contemporary Relevance

The Medicine Wheel continues to be a relevant and necessary aspect of Indigenous spirituality and cultural identity in contemporary times. Indigenous communities are actively working to preserve and revitalize their traditional teachings, including those related to the Medicine Wheel. These teachings offer valuable insights into living in harmony with the Earth, respecting all life, and seeking balance and spiritual growth. Furthermore, the principles of the Medicine Wheel have resonated with people from various cultural backgrounds who seek a deeper connection to the natural world and a greater understanding of their place within it. It has become a symbol of unity, enmeshment, and a shared commitment to caring for the Earth and its diverse inhabitants.

The Medicine Wheel is a sacred and universal symbol that includes the spiritual teachings of many Native American cultures. Its circular form, four directions, and central point serve as a guide for understanding life's cycles, the enmeshment of all things, and the presence of the Creator. The Medicine Wheel's teachings emphasize balance, harmony, and responsibility in one's adventure through life and continue to hold deep cultural and spiritual significance for Indigenous peoples and those who seek to learn from its wisdom.

XXXII: SIOUX STAR KNOWLEDGE

The Sioux tribes, including the Lakota, Dakota, and Nakota, have an opulent and profound tradition of astronomical knowledge and spiritual practices related to the stars. The night sky has always held great significance in Sioux culture, serving as a source of guidance, storytelling, and spiritual connection. Sioux Star Knowledge includes a deep understanding of celestial bodies, their movements, and their place in shaping the cultural and spiritual identity of the Sioux people.

The Sacredness of the Night Sky

For the Sioux tribes, the night sky is a sacred world that holds both practical and spiritual significance. The stars served as navigational aids, helping Sioux hunters and travelers find their way across the giant plains. However, the stars also carried deeper symbolic meanings, representing the spirits of ancestors and providing a connection to the Creator.

Star Constellations

Sioux Star Knowledge includes the recognition and interpretation of various star constellations. These constellations were not just used for practical purposes but also served as the basis for storytelling and cultural teachings. Different tribes within the Sioux Nation had their own unique constellations and narratives associated

with them. The Lakota, for example, have their own
distinct set of constellations and star knowledge.

The Seven Stars and the Seven Campfires

One of the most well-known celestial
elements in Sioux Star Knowledge is the "Seven
Stars" or the "Seven Sisters," which is a prominent
star cluster in the constellation Taurus. These stars
are known as the "Pleiades" in Western astronomy.
In Sioux culture, these stars are associated with the
"Seven Campfires" or "Seven Camp Circles." Each of
the Seven Sisters is said to represent a campfire, and
the entire cluster signifies the gathering of the seven
bands of the Lakota people. According to Lakota
tradition, the Lakota Nation was once divided into
seven distinct bands or subgroups. The Seven Sisters
constellation is a reminder of unity and the shared
heritage of the Lakota people.

The Morning Star and the Evening Star

Venus, often referred to as the Morning Star
or the Evening Star, holds special significance in
Sioux Star Knowledge. Venus is one of the brightest
objects in the night sky and can be seen either in the
east before sunrise (Morning Star) or in the west
after sunset (Evening Star). In Sioux culture, Venus is
associated with renewal and rebirth. Its appearance
in the morning symbolizes the dawn of a new day
and the opportunity for fresh beginnings. The
Evening Star, on the other hand, is associated with

the end of the day and reflection on one's actions and decisions. Both aspects of Venus are seen as important guides for personal and spiritual growth.

The Sun and Moon

The Sun and Moon hold central roles in Sioux cosmology. The Sun is often referred to as the "Wi" or "Wiyo," representing the life-giving force that provides warmth and sustenance to the Earth. The Moon, known as "Hanwi" or "Hanwi Wi," is associated with the female energy and is respected as a source of spiritual insight. The lunar cycle is particularly significant in Sioux culture, with each phase of the Moon carrying its own spiritual teachings and ceremonies. The New Moon, for example, stands for new beginnings, while the Full Moon is a time for celebration and reflection.

Eclipses and Celestial Events

Eclipses, meteor showers, and other celestial events were closely observed and interpreted by Sioux spiritual leaders and star knowledge keepers. These events were often seen as messages from the spirit world and were used to guide decisions, particularly regarding important tribal matters, hunting expeditions, or ceremonies. Solar eclipses, in particular, were regarded with great reverence and were seen as moments when the Sun and Moon came together in unity. Believed it was that during a solar eclipse, the spirits of ancestors could be more easily contacted, and ceremonies were conducted to honor and seek guidance from these spirits.

The Sacred Circle and the Medicine Wheel

The concept of the sacred circle is central to Sioux cosmology, and it is mirrored in the design of the Medicine Wheel, a ceremonial and spiritual structure. The Medicine Wheel is often aligned with specific celestial events, like the summer and winter solstices and the equinoxes, marking the changing seasons and the balance of life. Within the context of the Medicine Wheel, the stars and celestial bodies hold specific positions and symbolism, representing the enmeshment of all life and the ongoing cycle of birth, growth, maturity, and transformation.

Contemporary Relevance

Sioux Star Knowledge remains relevant in contemporary times, serving as a link to cultural identity, spirituality, and a deep connection to the natural world. Many Sioux people continue to honor and pass down their star knowledge through oral traditions, ceremonies, and cultural events. Furthermore, contemporary Sioux communities are actively engaged in efforts to preserve and revitalize their cultural heritage, including their astronomical traditions. Star knowledge workshops, storytelling sessions, and educational programs are conducted to ensure that the next generations can appreciate the significance of the stars and maintain their cultural identity.

Sioux Star Knowledge is a profound and multifaceted aspect of Sioux culture, encompassing practical navigation skills, storytelling, and spiritual connection. The stars, constellations, and celestial events serve as a bridge between the physical and spiritual worlds, offering guidance, wisdom, and a profound sense of enmeshment with the Creator and the natural world. As Indigenous communities strive to preserve their cultural heritage, Sioux Star Knowledge continues to shine brightly as an illuminant of cultural resilience and spiritual wisdom.

XXXIII: Mi'kmaq Hieroglyphics

The Mi'kmaq people, indigenous to the northeastern part of North America, have an opulent cultural and spiritual tradition that includes the use of hieroglyphic symbols in their written prayer books. These unique prayer symbols, known as "Mi'kmaq hieroglyphics" or "hieroglyphic writing," are a confirmation of the Mi'kmaq's deep connection with their spiritual beliefs, their reverence for the natural world, and their commitment to preserving their cultural heritage.

Origins and Development

Mi'kmaq hieroglyphics are one of the few known writing systems used by Indigenous peoples in North America prior to European contact. The origins of Mi'kmaq hieroglyphics can be traced back to ancient times, and it is believed to have evolved over centuries of use and adaptation. These symbols are not hieroglyphics in the traditional sense, as they do not represent individual sounds or letters like the ancient Egyptian hieroglyphs. Instead, they are ideographic symbols, meaning that each symbol conveys an entire concept, word, or phrase. Mi'kmaq hieroglyphics were primarily used in ceremonial contexts, particularly in the creation of prayer books and the recording of important spiritual knowledge.

The Symbolic Language

Mi'kmaq hieroglyphics include a wide range of symbols, each with its own specific meaning.

These symbols represent elements of the Mi'kmaq spiritual and cultural worldview, including animals, plants, natural phenomena, and human activities. The symbols are often stylized and simplified representations of the objects or concepts they represent. For example, the symbol for the "Eagle" consists of a simple representation of an eagle with its wings outstretched. Similarly, the symbol for "Bear" depicts a bear in a characteristic stance. These symbols go beyond mere representation; they embody the essence and spiritual significance of these creatures in Mi'kmaq culture.

Use in Prayer Books

Mi'kmaq hieroglyphics are most prominently featured in prayer books known as "bark books" or "wampum belts." These books are traditionally made from birch bark, and the hieroglyphics are etched or painted onto the bark using natural pigments. Wampum belts, made from beads and shells, also incorporate hieroglyphics as part of their complex designs.

These prayer books serve as repositories of spiritual knowledge, containing prayers, ceremonies, and teachings that are central to Mi'kmaq spirituality. The symbols are used to convey these teachings in a concise and symbolic manner, making them accessible to those who are initiated into the Mi'kmaq spiritual traditions.

Spiritual Significance

Mi'kmaq hieroglyphics are deeply founded in the spiritual beliefs of the Mi'kmaq people. Each symbol is a conduit for spiritual energy and wisdom, allowing individuals to connect with the spiritual world and receive guidance from the Creator and ancestral spirits. The act of creating or reading these symbols in prayer books is a sacred practice that requires deep reverence and concentration. It is believed that the symbols have the power to convey the intentions and prayers of the individual to the spirit world, facilitating communication with the Creator and the spirits.

Preserving Cultural Heritage

The use of Mi'kmaq hieroglyphics has been instrumental in preserving the cultural heritage of the Mi'kmaq people. These symbols are a unique and lasting confirmation of the resilience of Mi'kmaq culture in the face of colonialism and cultural assimilation efforts. Over the years, committed Mi'kmaq elders and knowledge keepers have worked tirelessly to pass down the knowledge of hieroglyphics to younger generations. Efforts have been made to document and record the meanings and usage of these symbols, ensuring that they are not lost to time.

Cultural Revival

In recent decades, there has been a revival of interest in Mi'kmaq hieroglyphics among the Mi'kmaq people and scholars alike. This resurgence is part of broader efforts to revitalize Mi'kmaq culture, language, and spirituality. Language and cultural programs have been established to teach Mi'kmaq hieroglyphics to new generations, and there is a growing appreciation for the spiritual and cultural significance of these symbols. Contemporary Mi'kmaq artists and artisans incorporate hieroglyphics into their work, bridging the gap between tradition and modern expression.

Challenges and Future Outlook

While there has been significant progress in preserving and revitalizing Mi'kmaq hieroglyphics, challenges remain. Many of the symbols and their meanings were not recorded in written form until relatively recently, and some knowledge may have been lost over the years. Efforts to document and standardize the symbols and their meanings are ongoing, and collaborations between Mi'kmaq communities and academic institutions have played an important place in this endeavor. The goal is to ensure that the symbols are accurately understood and transmitted to future generations.

In conclusion, Mi'kmaq hieroglyphics are a unique and spiritually significant form of written communication that reflects the deep connection between the Mi'kmaq people and their cultural and spiritual heritage. These symbols serve as a conduit for spiritual knowledge, allowing for communication with the Creator and ancestral spirits. As efforts to preserve and revitalize Mi'kmaq culture continue, hieroglyphics hold a necessary place in keeping alive the opulent traditions and spiritual teachings of the Mi'kmaq people.

XXXIV: Arikara Corn Mother Myth

The Arikara Corn Mother Myth is a spiritual narrative that dives into the origins of corn and underscores the deep reverence and importance of this staple crop in the culture and sustenance of the Arikara people. This myth is a confirmation of the connection between the Arikara tribe and the natural world, emphasizing their profound understanding of agriculture and the spiritual significance they attach to corn as a gift from the Creator.

The Gift of Corn

In the ancient days, when the world was still young and the Arikara people lived in harmony with the land, there came a time of great need. A harsh winter had taken its toll on the tribe, and food had become scarce. The people were hungry and worried about their survival. It was during this challenging time that a vision was granted to one of the Arikara elders.

The Vision

One evening, as the elder sat by the fire, meditating and seeking guidance from the Creator, a powerful vision enveloped him. In this vision, he saw a magnificent figure, a divine being, who radiated warmth and light. This being spoke to the elder with a voice as gentle as the wind and said, "Fear not, for I have heard your people's cries. I shall provide you with a gift, a sacred plant that will sustain your tribe and bless your lands." The elder was filled with awe and gratitude, for he respected that this divine being was the Corn Mother, the spirit of the corn itself. She stood before him, adorned with leaves and ears of corn, a living embodiment of the sacred crop.

The Corn Mother's Offering

The Corn Mother gestured for the elder to follow her. They walked together through the fields, and with each step, corn plants sprouted from the earth. The elder watched in wonder as the Corn Mother touched each plant, bestowing her blessings upon them. She taught the elder the ways of planting, cultivating, and harvesting corn, sharing the knowledge that would sustain the Arikara people for generations to come. As they continued their adventure, the Corn Mother explained that corn was a sacred gift from the Creator, a symbol of life, sustenance, and abundance. She revealed that each part of the corn plant held significance, starting from the kernels that represented the cycle of life to the leaves and husks that protected and nurtured the precious crop.

The Return to the Tribe

When the elder returned to the Arikara tribe, he carried with him the knowledge and blessings of the Corn Mother. He shared the details of his vision and the teachings he had received. The tribe listened with rapt attention, recognizing the importance of this sacred gift. With the guidance of the Corn Mother, the Arikara people planted the first cornfields, tended them with care, and witnessed the miraculous growth of this life-sustaining crop. Corn became a cornerstone of their culture, providing not just nourishment but also the foundation for ceremonies, rituals, and expressions of gratitude to the Creator.

The Spiritual Significance of Corn

In Arikara culture, corn is regarded as a sacred and life-giving plant. It symbolizes the benevolence of the Creator, who provides for the needs of the people. Each stage of corn's growth, from planting to harvesting, is accompanied by prayers and ceremonies that honor the Corn Mother and express gratitude for the abundance she bestows. Corn is often referred to as "Our Mother" or "Mother Corn" among the Arikara people, signifying the nurturing and life-giving qualities associated with this crop. The kernels of corn represent the cycle of birth, growth, and rebirth, mirroring the cycle of life in the natural world.

Cultural Practices and Ceremonies

The Arikara people incorporate corn into various cultural practices and ceremonies. The Green Corn Ceremony, for instance, is a significant annual event that marks the ripening of the first corn of the season. It is a time of purification, renewal, and thanksgiving. During this ceremony, the Arikara people gather to share a meal that includes freshly harvested corn. They offer prayers, sing songs, and express gratitude for the Creator's blessings. The Green Corn Ceremony reaffirms the spiritual connection between the Arikara people and corn and acts as a reminder of the sacred origins of this essential crop.

Heritage and Resilience

The Arikara Corn Mother Myth continues to be a central narrative in the cultural and spiritual life of the Arikara tribe. It underscores the tribe's lasting relationship with corn and their deep respect for the natural world. The myth reminds the Arikara people of their responsibility to protect and nurture the land and the crops it yields. In contemporary times, the Arikara people are actively involved in preserving their cultural heritage, including the cultivation of traditional corn varieties. Efforts are made to pass down the knowledge and ceremonies associated with corn to younger generations, ensuring the continuation of this sacred connection between the Arikara people, the Corn Mother, and the gift of corn.

The Arikara Corn Mother Myth is a piercing and undying narrative that speaks to the profound spiritual and cultural relationship between the Arikara people and corn. It acts as a confirmation of their resilience, reverence for the natural world, and gratitude for the life-sustaining gift bestowed upon them by the Corn Mother. This myth continues to be a source of encouragement and a guiding force in the cultural practices and spiritual life of the Arikara tribe.

XXXV: POMO BASKET WEAVING TRADITIONS

The Pomo people, indigenous to the northwestern region of California, have an opulent tradition of basket weaving that is not just a remarkable artistic endeavor but also a practice deeply intertwined with their spirituality, culture, and way of life. Pomo basketry stands as a confirmation of the skill, creativity, and profound connection between the Pomo people and the natural world. These complex baskets are not mere utilitarian objects but complex expressions of Pomo identity and spirituality.

Materials and Techniques

Pomo baskets are primarily made from local plant materials, with the most commonly used being willow, sedge root, redbud, and bulrush. Each of these materials has unique qualities that make them suitable for different aspects of basketry. Willow, for instance, provides the foundational structure, while sedge root is often used for complex designs and patterns. The weaving process is highly complex and time-consuming, involving a range of techniques, including coiling, twining, and plaiting. Pomo basket weavers demonstrate an extraordinary level of skill in manipulating these materials to create baskets of various shapes, sizes, and designs. The dexterity required for such complex work is a confirmation of the weavers' commitment and expertise.

Symbolism and Spirituality

Pomo baskets are not just functional objects but also carry deep spiritual and symbolic significance. The designs and patterns adorning these baskets are more than mere decoration; they are a form of visual storytelling and a means of communication. The motifs used often reflect elements of the natural world, like animals, plants, and landscapes, and convey the Pomo people's connection to their environment. Many Pomo baskets are adorned with sacred symbols that are believed to connect the physical and spiritual worlds. These symbols are passed down through generations and are used in ceremonies, rituals, and daily life. They serve as a reminder of the Pomo people's spiritual relationship with the land, animals, and the Creator.

The Connection to Nature

Pomo basketry is a reflection of the Pomo people's profound relationship with the natural world. Gathering the materials for basket weaving is a spiritual practice in itself, as it involves careful selection, preparation, and respect for the plants used. The Pomo people believe that the plants have their own spirits and that their use in basketry is a form of collaboration with the plant world. The act of weaving is seen as a way to honor the Creator and the enmeshment of all life. Pomo weavers often engage in prayers and rituals while weaving, infusing their baskets with positive energy and spiritual intentions. The finished baskets are respected as to be not just functional but also spiritually charged objects that bring harmony and balance to the home.

Baskets as Cultural Identity

Pomo baskets are an integral part of Pomo cultural identity. Each basket carries the unique artistic signature of the weaver, reflecting their personal style and creativity. These baskets are often given as gifts or used in traditional ceremonies and gatherings, serving as a means of cultural expression and preservation. The passing down of basket weaving skills from one generation to the next is a cherished tradition among the Pomo people. Elders hold a necessary place in teaching the art of basketry to younger generations, ensuring that this cultural practice continues to thrive.

Ceremonial and Ritual Use

Pomo baskets hold a significant place in various ceremonies and rituals. They are used as containers for sacred items and offerings during spiritual gatherings. The designs on the baskets are carefully chosen to align with the specific purpose of each ceremony, reinforcing the spiritual intentions behind the rituals. One well-known use of Pomo baskets is in the "Gift of the World" ceremony, which celebrates the harvest of acorns, a staple food of the

Pomo people. During this ceremony, baskets are filled with acorns and other traditional foods and are offered as gifts to the community, reinforcing the spirit of sharing and abundance.

Contemporary Revival and Challenges

In recent decades, there has been a renewed interest in Pomo basket weaving and a concerted effort to revitalize this traditional art form. Pomo weavers, along with cultural organizations and museums, are working to preserve and promote basketry traditions. Contemporary Pomo artists are also expanding the bounds of traditional basketry by incorporating modern materials and techniques while still honoring the core cultural and spiritual aspects. Challenges persist, however, as the availability of traditional materials becomes limited due to environmental changes and development. Additionally, the commercialization of Pomo baskets in the art market has led to issues of cultural appropriation and misrepresentation. Efforts are underway to address these challenges and protect the integrity of Pomo basketry.

Pomo basket weaving is a cultural and spiritual practice that embodies the deep connection between the Pomo people and the natural world. These complex baskets are not just objects of utility but also carriers of cultural identity, spirituality, and artistic expression. As the Pomo people continue to honor their traditions and adapt to contemporary challenges, their basketry stands as a symbol of resilience, creativity, and the lasting bond between humans and the environment.

XXXVI: SERI IRONWOOD CARVINGS

The Seri people, an indigenous group residing in the arid coastal region of Sonora, Mexico, possess a unique artistic tradition known as Seri Ironwood Carvings. These carvings, predominantly created from the dense, dark ironwood found in their desert homeland, serve as complex expressions of Seri cosmology, spirituality, and connection to the natural world. This art form includes the deep reverence the Seri have for their environment and reflects their lasting cultural identity.

Ironwood and Its Significance

The choice of ironwood as the primary medium for Seri carvings holds profound cultural significance. The Seri people call ironwood "comcaac" in their language, and it is highly esteemed for its density, durability, and resistance to decay. Ironwood trees are not just a necessary resource for the Seri, providing material for their carvings, but they are also seen as spiritual entities with their own significance in Seri cosmology. Ironwood trees are believed to have protective spirits that watch over the Seri people. This spiritual connection is integral to the carving process, as Seri artisans approach the trees with respect, offer prayers, and make offerings before harvesting the wood. The process of selecting and carving ironwood is thus imbued with spiritual intent, emphasizing the enmeshment between the Seri and their natural environment.

Cosmological Themes and Imagery

Seri Ironwood Carvings are distinguished by their complex designs and complex motifs, which often reflect elements of Seri cosmology and spirituality. These carvings frequently feature representations of animals, plants, celestial bodies, and mythical creatures, all of which hold symbolic and spiritual significance for the Seri people.

Animals

Animals hold a central place in Seri cosmology, representing not just physical beings but also spiritual entities. Certain animals are respected as protectors or spirit guides. For example, the sea turtle, known as "hant ihiit," is believed to carry the souls of the deceased to the afterlife. Seri carvings often depict sea turtles, embodying the spiritual adventure of the departed.

Celestial Bodies

The night sky holds a special place in Seri spirituality. The Seri are skilled astronomers and navigators, and their carvings often incorporate celestial bodies like stars and the moon. These symbols represent not just the physical aspects of the cosmos but also the spiritual connection between the Seri and the universe.

Mythical Creatures

Seri mythology is replete with tales of mythical creatures and spirits that inhabit the desert territory. These beings are both feared and revered, and their presence is acknowledged in Seri carvings. These creatures, like the "iisax," a shape-shifting being, and the "cahemic," a creature associated with bad omens, serve as reminders of the complex relationship between the natural and spiritual worlds.

Plants

Desert plants, including the famous saguaro cactus and the creosote bush, are often described in Seri carvings. These plants are not just essential for survival in the arid environment but are also imbued with spiritual significance. The saguaro cactus, for instance, is seen as a protector and provider of water and is often represented in Seri art.

Spiritual Rituals in Carving

Creating Seri Ironwood Carvings is a spiritual process that involves rituals, prayers, and offerings. The selection of the ironwood tree, the carving process itself, and the final product all carry sacred meaning. Seri artisans often work in solitude or with a small group, creating an atmosphere of reverence and concentration. Before carving, the artisan may begin on a spiritual adventure to connect with the spirit of the ironwood tree. They may offer traditional songs and prayers, seeking guidance and blessings. Each carving is seen as a collaboration between the artist and the spiritual world, with the resulting artwork carrying the energy and intentions of both.

Cultural Resilience and Revival

In recent decades, there has been a concerted effort to preserve and revitalize Seri Ironwood Carvings. Cultural organizations, artisans, and researchers have worked together to document and promote this unique art form. Initiatives have been launched to ensure that the knowledge and skills associated with carving are passed down to younger generations, strengthening the cultural continuity of the Seri people. At the same time, contemporary Seri artists are pushing the bounds of traditional ironwood carving by incorporating new techniques and materials while respecting the core spiritual and cultural aspects. This blend of tradition and innovation allows for the continued relevance of Seri Ironwood Carvings in the modern world.

Challenges and Conservation

Despite efforts to preserve this art form, there are challenges related to conservation. The ironwood tree, while abundant, faces threats from development and overharvesting. Conservation efforts are necessary to ensure the sustainable use of ironwood for carving while protecting the Seri people's natural environment.

In conclusion, Seri Ironwood Carvings are a profound expression of the Seri people's spirituality, cosmology, and cultural identity. These complex carvings serve as a bridge between the physical and spiritual worlds, embodying the enmeshment of the Seri with their natural environment and the spiritual entities that inhabit it. As the Seri work to preserve and revitalize their carving traditions, they continue to celebrate their cultural resilience and the lasting significance of their art.

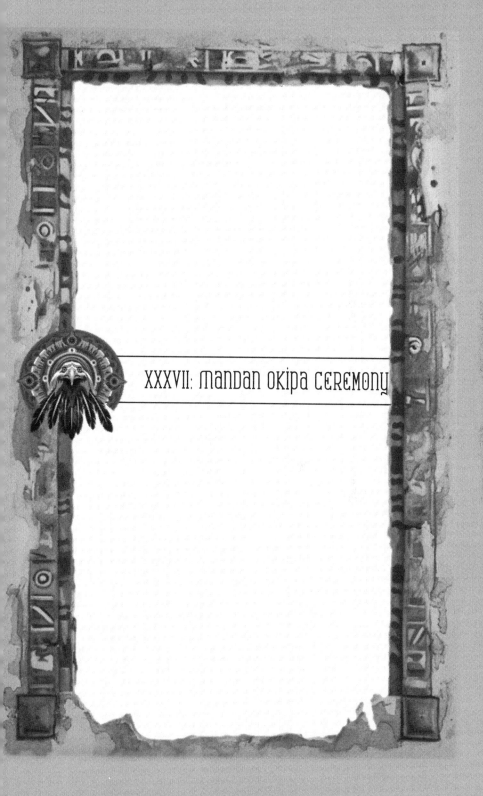

XXXVII: Mandan Okipa Ceremony

The Mandan Okipa Ceremony stands as one of the most complex, demanding, and spiritually significant rituals practiced by the Mandan people, a Native American tribe indigenous to the Great Plains region of North America. This ceremonial undertaking is a profound expression of Mandan cosmology, spirituality, and cultural identity. The Okipa Ceremony is a confirmation of the Mandan people's endurance, resilience, and deep connection to their ancestral traditions and the spiritual world.

Cultural and Historical Context:

The Mandan people are renowned for their complex social and ceremonial life. Their villages along the banks of the Missouri River were centers of cultural and spiritual activity. The Okipa Ceremony was a necessary event in the Mandan cultural calendar, typically held every four years, and served as a source of communal unity, spiritual renewal, and connection to the supernatural. The ceremony itself was an arduous and physically demanding undertaking, requiring extensive preparation and the participation of numerous individuals from the tribe. It combined elements of endurance, sacrifice, dance, and symbolic representation to engage with the spiritual world and seek blessings for the Mandan people.

Preparation and Initiation

The Okipa Ceremony involved months of careful preparation, with the entire community holding a place. The primary host of the ceremony, known as the Okipa Priest, held a central position and was responsible for overseeing the preparations, including the construction of a large ceremonial lodge, the procurement of necessary materials, and the selection of participants. Central to the ceremony was the initiation of young boys into adulthood. Boys who had reached a certain age were chosen to undergo the rigors of the Okipa as part of their rite of passage. This initiation marked their transition from childhood to adulthood and symbolized their readiness to assume the responsibilities of Mandan society.

Construction of the Okipa Lodge

One of the most visually striking aspects of the Okipa Ceremony was the construction of the massive Okipa Lodge, a structure built specifically for this ritual. The construction process itself was highly symbolic, with each element representing aspects of Mandan cosmology and spirituality.

The Okipa Lodge featured a distinctive circular design, with a central support pole symbolizing the world tree or axis mundi, connecting the physical and spiritual worlds. The circular layout also symbolized the cyclical nature of life and the enmeshment of all things. The lodge was adorned with sacred paintings, objects, and symbols that held spiritual significance for the Mandan people.

Sacrifice and Endurance

The Okipa Ceremony was characterized by acts of sacrifice and endurance by both the initiates and the participants. Central to the ceremony was the practice of self-inflicted pain and suffering as a means of demonstrating commitment, resilience, and spiritual commitment. Initiates would undergo piercing, a painful process in which wooden skewers or bone needles were inserted through the chest muscles. These skewers were then attached to ropes suspended from the lodge's central support pole. The initiates would dance and move in a way that caused the skewers to tug at their chest muscles, intensifying the pain. This act of self-sacrifice was believed to demonstrate the initiates' spiritual strength and their willingness to endure hardship for the benefit of their people.

Dance and Spiritual Connection

Dance was a central element of the Okipa Ceremony, with participants engaging in a series of highly choreographed and symbolic dances. The dance movements represented aspects of Mandan cosmology, including the adventure of the sun, the movement of animals, and the enmeshment of all living beings. The dancing was accompanied by sacred songs and chants, often performed by a designated group of singers. These songs conveyed the spiritual significance of the ceremony and served as a means of communication with the supernatural forces. The singing and dancing were believed to create a bridge between the physical and spiritual worlds, allowing the Mandan people to connect with their ancestors and seek blessings for the tribe.

Ceremonial Objects and Artifacts

The Okipa Ceremony featured a range of sacred objects and artifacts that held deep spiritual significance. These included sacred bundles, medicine bundles, and objects associated with specific clans or societies within the Mandan tribe. The placement and use of these objects were carefully orchestrated and symbolized the Mandan people's connection to their ancestral traditions and the spiritual world.

The Mandan Okipa Ceremony was a profoundly complex and spiritually significant ritual that encapsulated the Mandan people's cosmology, cultural identity, and endurance. This ceremonial undertaking served as a communal expression of spirituality, a rite of passage for young initiates, and a means of seeking blessings for the tribe. While the Okipa Ceremony is no longer practiced in its traditional form, it remains a confirmation of the resilience and cultural richness of the Mandan people. Efforts are underway to preserve and revitalize aspects of Mandan culture and spirituality, ensuring that the heritage of the Okipa Ceremony continues to be honored and understood by future generations.

XXXVIII: ŧewa people

The Tewa people, one of the Puebloan tribes native to the southwestern United States, possess an opulent and unique worldview deeply intertwined with their spirituality and cosmology. The Tewa worldview is characterized by a profound reverence for the natural world, a sense of enmeshment, and a commitment to maintaining harmony and balance in their lives. In exploring the spiritual beliefs and cosmology of the Tewa people, we gain insight into a culture that has endured for centuries, cherishing its deep-founded traditions and spiritual connection to the land.

The Sacred Territory

Central to the Tewa worldview is the recognition of the sacredness of their ancestral homelands. The Tewa people have lived for generations in the Rio Grande Valley and the surrounding mesas of northern New Mexico. They view the land as a living entity, replete with spiritual significance. The mountains, rivers, and forests are not just physical features but are inhabited by spirits, ancestors, and deities. For the Tewa, the connection to the land is more than geographical; it is deeply spiritual. Each natural feature is associated with specific spirits and has its own place in the Tewa cosmology. For example, the towering cliffs of their mesas are often seen as the dwelling places of powerful spirits, while the Rio Grande River is regarded as a life-giving force, providing sustenance and spiritual nourishment.

Katsina Traditions

One of the most recognizable aspects of Tewa spirituality is their reverence for Katsinam, also known as Kachinas. These spirits hold a central place in Tewa cosmology and are believed to be intermediaries between the human world and the divine. Katsinam are both benevolent and powerful, and they are celebrated through elaborate dances, ceremonies, and art forms. Katsina dances, known as "Katsina dances," are performed during specific times of the year. These dances are a means of inviting the Katsinam into the Tewa community to bless and guide them. Each Katsina has its own unique characteristics, roles, and attributes, representing aspects of the natural world and spiritual forces. The dances are highly symbolic and serve as a means of connecting with the spiritual world.

Cycles of Life and Agriculture

Agriculture plays a fundamental place in Tewa spirituality and cosmology. The Tewa people are skilled farmers who have cultivated the arid lands of the Southwest for centuries. Their agricultural practices are deeply founded in their spiritual beliefs.

The planting, growth, and harvest of crops are seen as sacred processes that mirror the cycles of life and the enmeshment of all living beings. The Tewa people offer prayers and perform rituals to honor the spirits of the land, seeking their guidance and blessings for a bountiful harvest. These agricultural rituals are not just practical but are also imbued with deep spiritual significance, reinforcing the idea that the Tewa people are stewards of the land.

Ceremonial and Ritual Life

Tewa ceremonial life is opulent and living, with a calendar filled with rituals and observances. These ceremonies are often tied to the agricultural calendar, celestial events, and the changing seasons. The Winter and Summer Solstices, for example, are significant times for the Tewa people and are marked by ceremonies that honor the sun and its place in sustaining life. Kiva ceremonies hold a special place in Tewa spirituality. The kiva, an underground chamber, acts as a sacred space for prayer, ritual, and communal gatherings. Kiva ceremonies are often private and are attended by members of specific societies or clans within the tribe. These ceremonies involve the use of sacred objects, songs, and prayers to connect with the spiritual world and seek guidance and blessings.

Ancestral and Clan Connections

The Tewa people maintain a strong connection to their ancestors and clans, which is integral to their cosmology and spirituality. Clans are organized groups within the tribe, each with its own set of responsibilities and spiritual affiliations. Clan members share a common lineage and are connected to specific aspects of Tewa cosmology. Ancestral knowledge is passed down through oral traditions, stories, and rituals. The Tewa people believe that their ancestors continue to watch over and guide them. Ceremonies often include offerings and prayers to honor and connect with these ancestral spirits.

Harmony and Balance

Central to Tewa spirituality is the concept of harmony and balance. The Tewa people strive to maintain equilibrium in all aspects of life, recognizing that disruptions can lead to disharmony and spiritual unrest. This commitment to balance extends to their relationship with the natural world, the spiritual world, and their interactions with one another. Tewa ceremonies, prayers, and rituals are designed to restore balance and harmony. When conflicts arise within the community or when illness occurs, ceremonies are conducted to bring healing and restoration. The Tewa people believe that by aligning themselves with the natural order and maintaining harmony in their lives, they can thrive spiritually and physically.

The Tewa worldview and spirituality offer profound insights into a culture deeply founded in its ancestral traditions and the land it calls home. The Tewa people's reverence for the sacred territory, their relationship with Katsinam, their agricultural practices, and their commitment to harmony and balance all reflect their profound connection to the natural and spiritual worlds. In preserving their traditions and sharing their cosmology, the Tewa people continue to celebrate their lasting cultural identity and spiritual heritage.

XXXIX: Caddo Nighttime Dances

The Caddo Nation, a Native American tribe located in the southeastern United States, has an opulent cultural and spiritual heritage that includes a tradition of nighttime dances. These ritual dances are central to Caddo spirituality and are opulent in spiritual meaning, serving as a means of connecting with the supernatural, preserving cultural traditions, and seeking blessings for the community. In exploring Caddo nighttime dances, we gain insight into the profound spiritual and cultural significance of these ceremonies.

Cultural and Historical Context

The Caddo people have a long history dating back thousands of years, with their ancestral homeland situated in what is now parts of Texas, Oklahoma, Arkansas, and Louisiana. Their cultural practices and spiritual traditions have evolved over the centuries, influenced by interactions with neighboring tribes and the challenges posed by European colonization. Caddo nighttime dances are deeply founded in the tribe's cultural identity and spiritual beliefs. These dances are traditionally performed at night, often during the warmer months, and are characterized by complex choreography, living regalia, and the rhythmic beating of drums. The dances provide a communal space for Caddo people to come together, express their spirituality, and celebrate their cultural heritage.

The Spiritual Significance of Nighttime Dances

Caddo nighttime dances hold profound spiritual meaning for the participants and the community as a whole. These dances are seen as a way to connect with the spiritual world, seek blessings, and maintain harmony within the tribe. Each dance has its own unique purpose and symbolism, reflecting different aspects of Caddo cosmology.

Corn Dances

One of the most important Caddo nighttime dances is the Corn Dance. This dance is committed to the spirit of corn, a staple crop that has sustained the Caddo people for generations. The Corn Dance is held to honor the corn's necessary place in their survival and to seek blessings for successful harvests. Participants wear regalia adorned with corn husks and leaves, and the dance is accompanied by songs and prayers that express gratitude to the spirit of corn.

Buffalo Dances

The Buffalo Dance is another significant Caddo nighttime dance that pays homage to the buffalo, a revered animal that once provided food, clothing, and shelter for the tribe. The dance is performed to honor the buffalo's spirit and to seek its return, as the buffalo herds had dwindled due to overhunting and environmental changes. Participants wear buffalo masks and regalia and mimic the movements of the buffalo in their dance, symbolizing their connection to this sacred animal.

Stomp Dances

Stomp dances are a series of Caddo dances performed in a square or circular formation. These dances are often held at night and are known for their energetic rhythms created by the participants' stomping feet and the beating of drums. Stomp dances serve various purposes, including celebrating important life events, seeking healing, and connecting with the spiritual world. The rhythmic energy of the dance is believed to invite the presence of benevolent spirits who can offer guidance and blessings.

Feast Dances

Feast dances are an integral part of Caddo nighttime ceremonies. These dances are performed as part of communal feasts, during which traditional foods are shared among the community. The dances serve as a way to express gratitude to the Creator for the abundance of food and to seek blessings for the wellness of the tribe. Participants often wear regalia adorned with symbols of food and agricultural abundance.

Masked Spirits and Ancestral Connections

Many Caddo nighttime dances feature masked dancers who represent spirits, deities, or ancestral beings. These masks are intricately crafted and hold deep spiritual significance. The masked dancers often take on the place of intermediaries between the human world and the spiritual world, conveying messages, offering blessings, and facilitating communication with the unseen forces. The use of masks in Caddo dances reinforces the tribe's connection to its ancestors and the belief that these spirits continue to watch over and guide their descendants. The masks also serve as a way to convey the sacredness of the dance and the presence of the spiritual world within the ceremony.

Community and Cultural Preservation

Caddo nighttime dances are more than just spiritual rituals; they are necessary components of community life and cultural preservation. These ceremonies provide opportunities for tribal members to come together, share their cultural traditions, and strengthen their sense of belonging to the Caddo Nation. The dances are passed down through generations, with elders holding an important place in teaching the songs, dances, and rituals to younger members. The Caddo Nation has faced challenges in preserving its cultural traditions due to factors like colonization, forced relocations, and the erosion of traditional knowledge. Despite these challenges, efforts are ongoing to revitalize and perpetuate Caddo cultural practices, including nighttime dances. Tribal leaders, cultural organizations, and community members work collaboratively to ensure the continued practice of these cherished traditions. Caddo nighttime dances represent a profound intersection of spirituality, culture, and community among the Caddo people. These dances serve as a means of connecting with the spiritual world, expressing gratitude, seeking blessings, and preserving cultural traditions. They are a confirmation of the lasting resilience and opulent cultural heritage of the Caddo Nation, reminding us of the importance of honoring and preserving indigenous spiritual practices and cultural expressions.

XL: Lakota Star Quilts

Lakota Star Quilts, also known as Star Blankets, are exquisite and highly symbolic textile creations deeply embedded in Lakota culture. These quilts are not just works of art; they are a profound expression of Lakota spirituality, worldview, and cultural identity. Through complex patterns and designs, Lakota Star Quilts convey profound spiritual themes, reflecting the Lakota people's connection to the universe and their ancestral traditions.

The history of Lakota Star Quilts is intertwined with the tumultuous events and cultural exchanges that occurred during the westward expansion of the United States. The Lakota, a Great Plains tribe, were renowned for their equestrian skills, warrior traditions, and artistic endeavors, including quillwork and beadwork. With the arrival of European settlers, trade goods like cloth and theme became more accessible, leading to the emergence of new art forms like quiltmaking.

Lakota Star Quilts are characterized by their complex geometric patterns, living colors, and, most importantly, their profound symbolism. These quilts are far more than decorative items; they convey spiritual messages and reflect Lakota cosmology and worldview. Some of the key spiritual themes represented in Lakota Star Quilts include:

The Universe

Central to Lakota spirituality is the belief in an interconnected universe. The star patterns on these quilts often represent the celestial world, with stars symbolizing celestial bodies and their spiritual significance. The Lakota people see themselves as part of this giant cosmic nexus, and the quilts serve as visual representations of their place in the universe.

Four Directions

The four cardinal directions—north, south, east, and west—hold immense significance in Lakota culture. These directions are often represented on the quilts through distinctive patterns and colors. Each direction is associated with specific spiritual qualities, elements, and sacred ceremonies. The quilt's design acts as a map of the spiritual and physical territory.

Balance and Harmony

Lakota Star Quilts often feature symmetrical designs that reflect the importance of balance and harmony in the Lakota way of life. The symmetry of the quilt's patterns mirrors the need for equilibrium between the physical and spiritual worlds and the enmeshment of all living beings.

Healing and Blessings

Quilts hold a place in Lakota healing ceremonies. They are believed to have protective and healing properties and are used to provide comfort and warmth to those in need. Gifting a quilt is an act of compassion, conveying blessings and goodwill to the recipient.

Quiltmaking Process

Creating a Lakota Star Quilt is a labor-intensive and highly skilled craft. Quilters carefully select fabrics, colors, and designs to convey specific spiritual messages and cultural meanings. The process typically involves several stages:

Design Selection

The choice of quilt design is a thoughtful and deliberate process. Patterns are often passed down through generations or may be encouraged by dreams and visions. Each design has its own spiritual significance.

Cutting and Piecing

Quilters cut and piece together fabric squares and triangles to create the quilt top. The precision of the piecing is important to achieving the desired symmetry and balance in the final design.

Appliqué and Stitching

Many Lakota Star Quilts feature appliqué work, where additional fabric pieces are sewn onto the quilt top to create complex patterns. The quilting stitches not just secure the layers of the quilt but also add texture and depth to the design.

Binding

A binding is added to the edges of the quilt to finish the piece and provide durability.

Cultural Significance

Lakota Star Quilts are more than just art; they are cultural treasures that convey a sense of identity, belonging, and continuity with ancestral traditions. These quilts are used in various life events, including weddings, births, and honoring ceremonies, and are often gifted to mark significant milestones in the lives of community members.

The act of gifting a Lakota Star Quilt is a gesture of respect, love, and spiritual connection. It symbolizes the giver's desire to share blessings, warmth, and protection with the recipient. The quilts serve as tangible expressions of community support and solidarity. In recent years, there has been a concerted effort to preserve and revitalize the art of Lakota Star Quiltmaking. Cultural organizations, artists, and quilters are working together to document traditional designs, pass down quilting techniques to younger generations, and ensure the continued practice of this sacred art form.

The revival of interest in Lakota Star Quilts has led to exhibitions, workshops, and collaborations with contemporary artists, resulting in the creation of innovative and stunning pieces that blend traditional motifs with modern interpretations.

Lakota Star Quilts are a confirmation of the lasting spirituality, creativity, and cultural richness of the Lakota people. These quilts serve as visual narratives of Lakota cosmology, connecting the physical and spiritual worlds through complex patterns and living colors. By preserving and sharing their quilting traditions, the Lakota people continue to celebrate their cultural identity and spiritual heritage, ensuring that the art of Lakota Star Quiltmaking remains a living and cherished part of their cultural heritage.

XLI: Salish Winter Spirit Dances

The Salish Winter Spirit Dances are profoundly significant ceremonial rituals performed by the Salish tribes, encompassing a group of indigenous peoples residing in the Pacific Northwest, particularly in regions spanning Montana, Idaho, Washington, and British Columbia. These sacred dances are conducted during the winter months and serve as a means of spiritual renewal, connecting with ancestral traditions, and seeking harmony and balance with the natural and supernatural worlds. To understand the depth of the Salish Winter Spirit Dances, it is essential to dive into their historical context, spiritual significance, and the complex elements that comprise these ceremonies.

Historical and Cultural Context

The Salish tribes have an opulent and diverse cultural heritage, with their history dating back thousands of years. Their ancestral territories include a wide range of landscapes, including mountains, forests, rivers, and coastal areas. This geographical diversity is mirrored in the diversity of their traditions and ceremonies, including the Winter Spirit Dances. These dances have been practiced for generations, passed down through oral traditions, songs, and rituals. They represent a living connection to the land, the seasons, and the spiritual beliefs of the Salish people. Despite the challenges posed by colonization and cultural assimilation, efforts are ongoing to preserve and revitalize the

Salish Winter Spirit Dances, ensuring that their cultural and spiritual significance endures.

Spiritual Renewal and Connection to the Seasons

The Salish Winter Spirit Dances are founded in the idea of spiritual renewal and the cyclical nature of life. Winter is a time when the natural world appears dormant, yet it is also a time of great spiritual activity for the Salish tribes. These dances are performed to honor and connect with the spirits of the winter season, seeking their blessings and guidance. Winter is seen as a time of reflection, purification, and preparation for the coming spring. The Salish people believe that during the winter months, the veil between the physical and spiritual worlds is thin, allowing for a closer connection with the spirits of the land, ancestors, and other supernatural beings. The Winter Spirit Dances are a way to strengthen this connection and receive spiritual insights.

Dance Styles and Regalia

The Salish Winter Spirit Dances include a variety of dance styles, each with its own unique movements, regalia, and symbolism. These dances are typically performed in a communal setting, with participants of all ages coming together to celebrate their spiritual traditions. Some of the notable dance styles include:

Buffalo Dance

The Buffalo Dance is a significant part of Salish winter ceremonies. It honors the buffalo, a symbol of abundance, strength, and survival for many indigenous peoples of the Great Plains. Dancers wear regalia adorned with buffalo symbols, like horns and hides, and mimic the movements of buffalo in their dance.

Coyote Dance

The Coyote Dance pays tribute to the clever and adaptable coyote, an important figure in Salish folklore. Dancers often wear coyote-themed regalia and engage in playful and humorous movements that capture the spirit of this famous animal.

Eagle Dance

The Eagle Dance is a powerful and graceful dance that honors the majestic eagle, a symbol of spirituality and vision for the Salish people. Dancers mimic the flight and hunting movements of eagles, wearing regalia adorned with eagle feathers and symbols.

Squirrel Dance

The Squirrel Dance celebrates the industrious and resourceful squirrel, which is revered for its ability to prepare for the winter months. Dancers embody the playful and agile nature of squirrels, often incorporating acrobatic movements into the dance.

The rhythmic beating of drums and the melodic singing of songs are integral components of the Salish Winter Spirit Dances. Drum groups, consisting of singers and drummers, provide the musical accompaniment for the dances. The songs are sung in the Salish language and convey spiritual messages, stories, and prayers. The drumbeat acts as a heartbeat, connecting the dancers to the earth and the pulse of the spiritual world. The songs are passed down through generations and are respected as sacred. They evoke a sense of reverence, unity, and spiritual harmony among the participants.

Community and Healing

The Salish Winter Spirit Dances encourage a sense of community and belonging among the participants. These ceremonies provide an opportunity for individuals and families to come together, share their cultural traditions, and strengthen their bonds with one another. They also serve as occasions for healing and spiritual guidance. The dances are sometimes accompanied by rituals like smudging with sage, a purification practice that cleanses participants and the ceremonial space. The act of dancing and singing in harmony with the natural world is believed to bring healing and balance to the community, both individually and collectively.

The Salish Winter Spirit Dances represent a profound expression of Salish spirituality, cultural identity, and connection to the natural and supernatural worlds. These ceremonies embody the cyclical nature of life, the reverence for the seasons, and the lasting spiritual traditions of the Salish tribes. As efforts continue to preserve and revitalize these dances, the Salish people ensure that their cultural and spiritual heritage remains living and cherished, encouraging a deep connection to their ancestral traditions and the land they call home.

XLII: OSAGE ORIGIN STORIES

The Osage Nation, a Native American tribe originally from the Ohio Valley, possesses an opulent atlas of origin stories and spiritual narratives that are deeply ingrained in their cultural and spiritual identity. These stories are not just historical accounts; they are profound expressions of the Osage worldview, cosmology, and the spiritual relationship between the Osage people and the natural world. To truly understand the significance of Osage origin stories, one must dive into their historical context, the themes they include, and their lasting importance in Osage culture.

Historical Context

The Osage Nation, known as the "Children of the Middle Waters," has a complex and ancient history that spans millennia. Originally inhabiting the Ohio Valley region, the Osage migrated westward over the centuries, settling in what is now the states of Missouri, Arkansas, Kansas, and Oklahoma. Their history is marked by interactions with other tribes, European explorers, and the challenges posed by westward expansion.

Creation and Origin Stories

The Osage possess a variety of origin stories that explain the creation of the world and the emergence of their people. These stories are typically passed down through oral traditions, preserving the cultural and spiritual heritage of the tribe. While specific details may vary among different Osage communities and clans, common themes run through their origin narratives:

The Emergence

One of the central themes in Osage origin stories is the concept of "emergence." According to Osage belief, the world was initially covered by water, and the first people emerged from a subterranean world through a cave or hole. This emergence stands for not just the physical birth of the Osage people but also their spiritual connection to the earth and the cosmos.

The Animal People

In many Osage origin stories, the Animal People hold a significant place. These mythical beings are often portrayed as benevolent guides who help the emerging Osage people by providing knowledge, cultural teachings, and spiritual guidance. The Animal People are seen as the Osage's earliest ancestors, and their attributes and characteristics are mirrored in Osage clan systems.

The Sacred Bundle

The concept of the Sacred Bundle is central to Osage spirituality and origin stories. The Sacred Bundle is a collection of sacred objects, stories, songs, and rituals that embody the essence of Osage identity and culture. It is believed to have been given to the Osage people by the Creator and contains the wisdom and traditions of the tribe. The care and maintenance of the Sacred Bundle are entrusted to specific tribal members who hold essential roles in preserving and perpetuating Osage spirituality.

Spiritual Significance

Osage origin stories are not mere legends but profound spiritual narratives that underpin Osage culture and worldview. They convey several key spiritual and cultural themes:

Connection to the Land

The Osage origin stories emphasize the deep connection between the Osage people and the land they inhabit. The emergence from the earth underscores their belief in a spiritual and physical bond with the natural world.

Ancestral Continuity

The stories of the Animal People and the emergence serve as a reminder of the lasting presence of ancestors in Osage life. Ancestral wisdom, teachings, and values are passed down through generations, ensuring cultural continuity.

Harmony and Balance

Osage spirituality is centered on the principles of balance and harmony. The stories emphasize the importance of living in balance with the natural world, respecting the spirits of the land and the animals, and maintaining spiritual equilibrium.

Cultural Identity

The Sacred Bundle, as a symbol of Osage identity and cultural continuity, reinforces the importance of preserving and passing down traditional knowledge, ceremonies, and practices. It acts as a source of cultural pride and a guide for Osage individuals and communities.

Ceremonial Practices

Osage origin stories are intimately tied to the tribe's ceremonial practices and rituals. The stories provide the foundation for many Osage ceremonies, including the In-Lon-Schka (Hun-Kah) dances, the Pawhuska In-Lon-Schka, and the Tzi-Zho Wash-Ka-Mo. These ceremonies are essential for maintaining spiritual balance, seeking blessings, and celebrating Osage culture. The In-Lon-Schka dances, in particular, are a significant part of Osage life. These dances are performed annually and are committed to the ancestors, the Creator, and the wellness of the Osage people. Participants wear traditional regalia, and the dances are accompanied by songs and rituals that reflect the themes and teachings of Osage origin stories.

Preservation and Revitalization

The preservation and revitalization of Osage origin stories are ongoing efforts within the Osage Nation. Tribal elders and cultural leaders hold an important place in passing down these narratives to younger generations. Additionally, written records and documentation help ensure that the stories are accessible to future Osage generations. Contemporary Osage individuals and communities continue to get in touch with their origin stories as sources of cultural pride and spiritual guidance. Efforts to revitalize Osage language, traditions, and ceremonies are integral to preserving the profound spiritual heritage embedded in these narratives.

Osage origin stories are the spiritual and cultural foundation of the Osage Nation. They represent the deep connection between the Osage people, the land, and the spiritual world. These narratives convey profound lessons about balance, harmony, and cultural identity, serving as a source of encouragement and guidance for the Osage people as they navigate the challenges of the modern world while preserving their opulent cultural heritage and spiritual traditions.

XLIII: CHEROKEE BOOGER DANCE

The Cherokee Booger Dance, also known as the Booger Mask Dance, is a traditional Cherokee ceremony that holds great cultural and spiritual significance. This dance is characterized by the use of complex masks and regalia, as well as a cast of masked figures representing various characters from Cherokee mythology. The Booger Dance is a living and complex cultural expression that serves both spiritual and social purposes within the Cherokee community. To truly appreciate the depth and significance of the Booger Dance, one must dive into its historical context, the symbolism of the masks, and the ceremonial aspects that make it a unique and cherished tradition among the Cherokee people. The Cherokee Nation, one of the largest indigenous nations in the southeastern United States, has an opulent cultural heritage that includes a diverse range of ceremonial practices and traditions. The Booger Dance is one such tradition that has been passed down through generations. Its origins are deeply founded in Cherokee history and spirituality.

The Booger Dance is believed to have originated as a part of the Cherokee Stomp Dance complex, a series of dances that hold a central place in Cherokee religious and social life. Over time, the Booger Dance developed its unique identity and significance within Cherokee culture.

At the heart of the Booger Dance are the masks worn by the participants. These masks are intricately crafted and represent a wide array of characters from Cherokee mythology and folklore. Each mask has its own distinct design, colors, and features, which convey specific meanings and identities. Some of the common characters represented in the Booger Dance include:

Boogers

The term "Booger" refers to a class of mischievous or supernatural beings in Cherokee mythology. Boogers are often described as hairy, wild creatures with distinctive features. They can take on various roles within the dance, from jesters and tricksters to protectors and intermediaries with the spirit world.

Wild animals

Masks representing animals like bears, wolves, and birds are also part of the Booger Dance. These animal figures embody the spiritual qualities and characteristics associated with these creatures in Cherokee cosmology.

Clowns and jesters

Some masks portray comical and whimsical characters, adding an element of humor and levity to the dance. These figures engage in playful antics and interactions with other dancers.

Spiritual beings

Masks representing spiritual beings, like spirits of the ancestors or divine entities, are an integral part of the Booger Dance. They connect the dancers to the spiritual world and convey blessings and guidance.

Each mask is respected as a work of art and is carefully passed down through families or created by skilled artisans within the Cherokee community. The creation and maintenance of these masks are sacred responsibilities, and the masks themselves are treated with great reverence.

The Booger Dance is typically performed in the evening or at night, under the light of a campfire or torches. The dance takes place in a circular or square arena, with the dancers moving in a counterclockwise direction. The music is provided by a group of singers and drummers who accompany the dance with rhythmic songs and chants. The dance is a lively and energetic affair, with each masked character holding a specific place. Boogers may engage in humorous interactions with the audience and other dancers, creating an atmosphere of both reverence and mirth. The dance may include symbolic actions, like the sweeping of the arena with pine branches, which is believed to purify the space and invite the presence of spirits.

Throughout the performance, the masks serve as a conduit between the physical and spiritual worlds. The dancers, in their roles as Boogers and other characters, facilitate communication with the spirit world, convey blessings to the community, and ensure the wellness of the Cherokee people.

Spiritual Significance

The Booger Dance holds profound spiritual significance for the Cherokee people. It acts as a means of connecting with ancestral spirits, seeking guidance from the spirit world, and maintaining harmony within the community. Some of the spiritual aspects of the Booger Dance include:

Ancestral Connection

The masks worn by the dancers connect them to their ancestors and the wisdom of past generations. The dance is a way of honoring and remembering those who came before and seeking their blessings.

Balance and Harmony

The Booger Dance embodies the Cherokee belief in the importance of balance and harmony in all aspects of life. The dance itself is a reflection of the balance between seriousness and humor, the natural and supernatural, and the physical and spiritual worlds.

Protection and Healing

Boogers and other masked characters are often seen as protectors of the community. Their presence in the dance is believed to ward off negative influences and bring healing and wellness to the Cherokee people.

Cultural Continuity

The Booger Dance acts as a necessary link to Cherokee cultural identity and traditions. It is an expression of Cherokee resilience and a confirmation of the preservation of their cultural heritage despite historical challenges.

The Booger Dance is not just a spiritual ceremony; it also serves important social functions within the Cherokee community. It brings people together, encourages a sense of unity and belonging, and strengthens social bonds. The dance often includes a communal feast, where traditional Cherokee foods are shared, and community members come together to celebrate their cultural identity. Furthermore, the Booger Dance provides an opportunity for younger generations to learn about their heritage and participate in the traditions of their ancestors. Elders hold an important place in passing down the knowledge and teachings associated with the dance, ensuring its continuity.

The Cherokee Booger Dance is a living and multifaceted cultural and spiritual tradition that embodies the essence of Cherokee identity and spirituality. Through the masks and characters of the dance, the Cherokee people connect with their history, their ancestors, and the spiritual world. It is a living confirmation of the resilience and lasting cultural heritage of the Cherokee Nation, reflecting their commitment to preserving and celebrating their opulent traditions in the face of historical challenges. The Booger Dance continues to be a cherished and revered ceremony that plays a central place in the cultural and spiritual life of the Cherokee people.

XLIV: OJIBWA dREAM CATCHER

The Ojibwa Dream Catcher, also known as the Anishinaabe or Chippewa Dream Catcher, is a traditional and famous symbol of indigenous North American culture, particularly associated with the Ojibwa people. These complex and beautifully crafted objects have transcended their cultural origins to become widely respected and admired symbols of spirituality and protection. The Dream Catcher's origin is deeply founded in Ojibwa legend and spirituality, and its design and purpose have evolved over time. To truly appreciate the significance of the Ojibwa Dream Catcher, it is essential to adventure through its historical context, its place in Ojibwa culture, and the lasting symbolism it holds in both indigenous and mainstream societies. The Ojibwa, also known as the Anishinaabe or Chippewa, are an indigenous people of North America, primarily residing in the northern regions of the United States and Canada, including the Great Lakes area and the surrounding woodlands. Their culture is opulent in traditions, storytelling, and spirituality, all of which are deeply intertwined with the natural world.

The Dream Catcher has its foundations in Ojibwa legend and mythology. While its precise origin story may vary among different Ojibwa communities and storytellers, a common theme in these legends is the concept of protection from negative or harmful dreams. The Dream Catcher's design and purpose have evolved over time, but its cultural significance remains strong within the Ojibwa and other indigenous communities. The traditional Ojibwa Dream Catcher consists of a circular frame made of willow or other flexible branches, forming a hoop that stands for the nexus of life. The frame is often adorned with decorative elements, like feathers, beads, and leather, that hold their own cultural and spiritual significance. At the center of the circular frame, a charted net or nexus is created using a material like sinew or twine. This nexus is intricately designed to resemble a spider's nexus, and its construction is symbolic of the enmeshment of all living beings. The central hole of the nexus allows positive dreams to pass through while trapping negative ones.

The Dream Catcher's spiritual significance is profound and multifaceted. It is founded in Ojibwa beliefs about dreams, spirits, and the enmeshment of all life. Some of the key spiritual aspects of the Ojibwa Dream Catcher include:

Protection from Negative Dreams

The primary purpose of the Dream Catcher is to protect the sleeper from negative or harmful dreams. In Ojibwa belief, dreams are powerful and can carry both positive and negative energy. The Dream Catcher is thought to capture and filter out negative dreams, allowing only positive and meaningful dreams to pass through the central hole and enter the sleeper's consciousness.

Connection to Spider Woman

Many Ojibwa legends attribute the creation of the Dream Catcher to Spider Woman, a spiritual and benevolent figure who watches over and guides the Ojibwa people. The complex nexus design of the Dream Catcher is often seen as a representation of Spider Woman's protective presence.

Cultural Continuity

The Dream Catcher acts as a symbol of cultural continuity and preservation among the Ojibwa and other indigenous communities. Its existence and continued use convey a commitment to maintaining and celebrating traditional practices in the face of historical challenges and cultural assimilation.

Enmeshment

The circular shape of the Dream Catcher and the interconnected strands of the nexus symbolize the enmeshment of all living beings and the cyclical nature of life. It reminds individuals of their place within the larger nexus of existence and the responsibilities that come with it.

Contemporary and Cross-Cultural Significance

The Ojibwa Dream Catcher has transcended its cultural origins to become a globally respected and cherished symbol. Its aesthetic beauty, coupled with its spiritual connotations, has made it a popular item in various settings, including art, home decor, and fashion. Dream Catchers are often seen in homes, offices, and even as tattoos, where they are believed to bring protection and positive energy. However, it's important to note that the commercialization and mass production of Dream Catchers have raised concerns among indigenous communities about cultural appropriation and the misrepresentation of their sacred traditions. Many Ojibwa and other indigenous artisans continue to create authentic Dream Catchers while also advocating for cultural respect and understanding.

The Ojibwa Dream Catcher is a symbol of deep cultural and spiritual significance that has transcended its origins to become a beloved and recognizable icon. Its design and purpose reflect the Ojibwa worldview, emphasizing the importance of protection from negative influences, the enmeshment of all life, and the preservation of indigenous traditions. While its image has become ever-present in popular culture, it is essential to remember and honor the cultural foundations and spiritual significance of the Dream Catcher, respecting its origins and the communities to which it belongs.

XLV: YUROK REDWOOD PLANK HOUSES

The Yurok people, native to the northwestern coast of California, have an opulent cultural and spiritual heritage deeply intertwined with their natural surroundings. Among the many aspects of Yurok culture, their traditional Redwood Plank Houses hold great spiritual significance. These unique and famous structures are not just architectural marvels but also embody the Yurok worldview, their relationship with the land, and their spiritual connection to the environment. To truly appreciate the depth of Yurok Redwood Plank Houses' spiritual significance, it is essential to adventure through their historical context, cultural symbolism, and lasting importance within Yurok society.

The Yurok people have inhabited the region along the Klamath River in northwestern California for thousands of years, relying on the opulent natural resources of the area for sustenance and cultural expression. The Yurok culture places a strong emphasis on living in harmony with the land and the spiritual world. Their traditions, stories, and ceremonies are deeply founded in their relationship with the environment.

Yurok Redwood Plank Houses, known as ' 'uuroy in the Yurok language, have been an integral part of Yurok culture for generations. These traditional houses served as places of shelter, gathering, and spiritual practice. The construction of Redwood Plank Houses reflects the Yurok people's profound understanding of their natural surroundings and their deep respect for the redwood trees, which are often referred to as "the ancestors" in Yurok cosmology.

Yurok Redwood Plank Houses are unique in their architectural design and construction. They are typically built using large redwood planks, with an elongated, rectangular shape. The walls are often adorned with intricately carved and painted designs that hold spiritual and cultural significance. Key elements of their design and symbolism include:

Redwood as Ancestors

The use of redwood trees in the construction of these houses is not merely practical; it is deeply symbolic. The Yurok people view redwoods as living ancestors, and the act of harvesting and using redwood for their homes is a spiritual and respectful endeavor. This connection to the redwoods reflects the Yurok belief that all life is interconnected.

Rectangular Shape

The elongated rectangular shape of Redwood Plank Houses is symbolic of the Yurok worldview. It stands for the balance and harmony searched out in Yurok culture, mirroring the natural world's order and balance. The rectangular shape also allows for communal gatherings, ceremonies, and the practice of traditional dances.

Complex Carvings and Paintings
The walls of Redwood Plank Houses are often adorned with elaborate carvings and paintings. These designs depict Yurok cosmology, spiritual stories, and the natural world. They serve as a visual representation of the Yurok relationship with the land and the spirits that inhabit it.

Spiritual Significance
Yurok Redwood Plank Houses have profound spiritual significance within Yurok culture. They are respected as sacred spaces where spiritual ceremonies, rituals, and gatherings take place. Some of the key aspects of their spiritual significance include:

Ceremonial Space
These houses serve as sacred spaces for various Yurok ceremonies and rituals, like the Brush Dance, the World Renewal Ceremony, and other traditional dances and spiritual practices. The houses are carefully prepared and cleansed before these ceremonies to ensure their spiritual purity.

Connection to Ancestors
The use of redwood, believed to be the ancestors, in the construction of the houses creates a direct link between the physical world and the spiritual world. Yurok people believe that their

ancestors watch over them and guide them from within these houses.

Communal Gathering

Redwood Plank Houses are centers of community life. They provide a place for communal gatherings, storytelling, and the passing down of traditional knowledge from one generation to the next. The sense of community and shared spirituality is palpable within these sacred spaces.

Harmony with Nature

The houses reflect the Yurok people's commitment to living in harmony with nature. The use of sustainable materials and the respect for the redwood trees emphasize the Yurok's belief in the enmeshment of all life forms.

While the Yurok Redwood Plank Houses have deep historical and spiritual foundations, they continue to hold significance in contemporary Yurok culture. Efforts are being made to preserve and revitalize these traditional structures and the ceremonies associated with them. Tribal members are learning the skills necessary for constructing and maintaining Redwood Plank Houses, ensuring the continuity of their cultural heritage.

Furthermore, the Yurok people are actively engaged in cultural revitalization efforts, including language revitalization, traditional dance and song preservation, and the transmission of cultural knowledge to younger generations. Redwood Plank Houses hold a necessary place in these efforts by providing a physical and spiritual space for cultural practices. Yurok Redwood Plank Houses are more than just architectural wonders; they are sacred spaces that embody the spiritual connection between the Yurok people and their environment. These houses reflect the Yurok worldview, their relationship with the land, and their deep respect for the redwood trees. They continue to serve as centers of community life, places of spiritual practice, and symbols of cultural resilience and preservation. The Yurok Redwood Plank Houses are a confirmation of the lasting spiritual and cultural heritage of the Yurok people and their commitment to passing down their traditions to future generations.

XLVI: Haudenosaunee

Great Law of Peace

The Haudenosaunee, often known as the Iroquois Confederacy, possess a unique and lasting system of governance and spirituality encapsulated in the Great Law of Peace. This remarkable constitution has not just shaped the political territory of the Haudenosaunee nations but also offers profound insights into their spiritual beliefs and their harmonious relationship with the natural world. The Great Law of Peace, which predates the founding of the United States and continues to guide the Haudenosaunee to this day, stands as a confirmation of the wisdom and lasting strength of indigenous governance and spirituality.

The Haudenosaunee Confederacy, comprising the Mohawk, Oneida, Onondaga, Cayuga, and Seneca nations, is one of the oldest participatory democracies in the world. Long before the arrival of European settlers, the Haudenosaunee had established a complex system of governance based on principles of peace, unity, and consensus. The Great Law of Peace, also known as Gayanashagowa, served as the spiritual and political foundation of this confederacy.

The origins of the Great Law of Peace are deeply founded in Haudenosaunee oral tradition, making it challenging to pinpoint its exact historical development. However, it is believed to have been formulated in the late 12th or early 13th century by the legendary figures Hiawatha and the Peacemaker, who searched out to bring an end to intertribal warfare and establish a scaffolding for peaceful coexistence.

The Great Law of Peace is built upon a set of fundamental principles that guide both the governance and spirituality of the Haudenosaunee. These principles are central to understanding the depth and significance of the Great Law:

Peace and Unity

The foremost principle of the Great Law is the pursuit of peace and unity among the member nations. It focuses on the importance of resolving conflicts through diplomacy, dialogue, and consensus, rather than through violence or coercion.

Consensus Decision-Making

The Haudenosaunee Confederacy operates on a system of consensus decision-making, where each nation has equal representation and a voice in matters of governance. This ensures that decisions are made collectively and reflect the will of the entire confederacy.

Non-Coercion

The Great Law prohibits the use of force or coercion in any form. It underscores the importance of respecting individual autonomy and the sovereignty of each nation within the confederacy.

Nature and Spirituality
The Haudenosaunee have a deep spiritual connection to the natural world. The Great Law recognizes the place of the natural world in guiding human behavior and decision-making. It focuses on living in harmony with the environment and respecting all living beings.

Individual and Collective Responsibility
The Great Law places equal emphasis on individual and collective responsibility. It encourages individuals to uphold the principles of peace, while also holding the collective accountable for maintaining the harmony of the confederacy.

Spiritual Significance
The Great Law of Peace is not merely a political constitution; it is intrinsically linked to Haudenosaunee spirituality. The spiritual aspects of the Great Law include:

The Peacemaker's Vision
The story of the Peacemaker's vision and mission to unite the nations under the Great Law is a central component of Haudenosaunee spirituality. It is believed that the Peacemaker was guided by the Creator to bring the message of peace and unity to the people.

Sacred Symbols

The Great Law incorporates sacred symbols, like the Tree of Peace, the Longhouse, and the Wampum Belt, which hold deep spiritual significance. These symbols serve as reminders of the core principles and the spiritual foundations of the confederacy.

Ceremonies and Rituals

The Haudenosaunee conduct various ceremonies and rituals to honor the Great Law and seek guidance from the spiritual world. These ceremonies often involve offerings, songs, dances, and the use of wampum belts to convey messages and agreements.

The Natural World

Haudenosaunee spirituality is intricately tied to the natural world. The Great Law focuses on the sacredness of all living beings, the elements, and the land itself. This spiritual connection underscores the responsibility to care for and protect the environment.

Oral Tradition

The Great Law is primarily passed down through oral tradition, with appointed leaders known as wampum keepers responsible for preserving and reciting its teachings. This oral transmission ensures that the spiritual essence of the Great Law endures.

The Great Law of Peace remains a necessary and relevant document for the Haudenosaunee Confederacy in the modern era. It continues to guide their governance and acts as an illuminant of indigenous sovereignty and self-determination. In recent years, the Haudenosaunee have used the principles of the Great Law to assert their rights in matters of land, resources, and cultural preservation.

Moreso, the Great Law of Peace has encouraged discussions about governance, diplomacy, and conflict resolution on a global scale. Its emphasis on consensus decision-making, non-coercion, and environmental stewardship offers valuable lessons for addressing contemporary challenges.

The Great Law of Peace stands as a confirmation of the lasting wisdom of the Haudenosaunee people. It is a spiritual and political constitution that has guided their governance, upheld their values of peace and unity, and preserved their cultural heritage for centuries. The principles of the Great Law continue to inspire indigenous communities, scholars, and advocates worldwide, emphasizing the importance of spirituality, consensus, and respect for the natural world in shaping a just and harmonious society.

XLVII: ZUNI SHALAKO FESTIVAL

The Zuni Shalako Festival, also known as the Shalako Ceremony, stands as one of the most significant and revered cultural and spiritual events among the Zuni people, a Native American tribe located in western New Mexico. Founded in ancient traditions and beliefs, the Shalako Festival is a multi-day ceremony that marks the conclusion of the Zuni calendar year and the welcoming of a new one. This celebration is characterized by the appearance of elaborately costumed figures, known as Shalako, who represent powerful ancestral beings and bring blessings to the Zuni community. To truly appreciate the depth of spiritual and cultural importance of the Zuni Shalako Festival, one must adventure through its historical context, the symbolism of the Shalako figures, the complex rituals involved, and its significance within the broader Zuni worldview.

The Zuni people have an opulent and ancient cultural heritage that dates back for thousands of years in the southwestern United States. Their unique customs, beliefs, and practices have been passed down through generations, and the Shalako Festival is a prime example of their lasting cultural traditions. The origins of the Shalako Festival are deeply intertwined with Zuni mythology and cosmology. It is believed to have been established by the Zuni's ancestral beings and is regarded as a sacred obligation to uphold. The festival also acts as a way to connect the Zuni people with their ancestors, the natural world, and the spiritual world.

At the heart of the Shalako Festival are the Shalako figures themselves. These figures represent ancestral beings who are essential to Zuni cosmology and spirituality. The Shalako figures are intricately crafted wooden sculptures adorned with feathers, turquoise, and other symbolic elements. They embody a powerful presence and are respected as intermediaries between the Zuni people and the spiritual world. Each Shalako figure stands for a specific ancestral being, and their arrival during the festival is seen as a spiritual event. The Shalako figures are divided into two main groups: the male Shalako, known as the Shalako Mana, and the female Shalako, known as the Shalako Watsi. Their distinct appearances and roles hold deep symbolism within Zuni culture.

The Shalako Festival is a multi-day event filled with complex rituals and ceremonies. It typically takes place in late November or early December, marking the end of the Zuni calendar year and the beginning of a new one. The festival's main elements include:

Preparation

Months of preparation precede the Shalako Festival. Zuni families work together to craft the Shalako figures, creating elaborate costumes and adorning them with feathers, jewelry, and other symbolic elements.

Kiva Blessings

The festival begins with blessings and rituals in the Zuni kivas, underground chambers used for spiritual ceremonies. These kiva ceremonies are essential for purifying the Shalako figures and preparing them for their adventure.

Dances and Processions

The Shalako figures, carried by skilled dancers, make their way through the Zuni pueblo, visiting the homes of various community members. These processions involve complex dances and chants performed by the Zuni people, offering blessings and receiving blessings in return.

Gift-Giving

The Shalako figures are presented with gifts, including food, blankets, and other offerings, by community members. This exchange of gifts symbolizes reciprocity and gratitude.

Fire Ceremonies

Fire ceremonies are an integral part of the Shalako Festival. Bonfires are lit to provide warmth and light during the winter season, and the sacred fire is used for various purification rituals.

Prayers and Blessings

Throughout the festival, prayers and blessings are offered to ensure the wellness and prosperity of the Zuni community in the coming year. These prayers are directed toward the Shalako figures, who are believed to carry the hopes and wishes of the people.

The Zuni Shalako Festival holds profound spiritual and cultural significance within the Zuni community:

Harmony and Renewal

The festival symbolizes the renewal of life and the restoration of balance and harmony within the Zuni world. It is a time for reflecting on the past year's challenges and celebrating the potential for a prosperous future.

Connection to Ancestors

The Shalako figures serve as a connection to the Zuni ancestors and the spiritual world. They are seen as benevolent beings who bring blessings, protection, and guidance to the community.

Cultural Preservation

The Shalako Festival is a confirmation of the preservation of Zuni cultural traditions. It reinforces the importance of passing down ancestral knowledge, craftsmanship, and spiritual practices to future generations.

Community Unity

The festival encourages a sense of unity and solidarity within the Zuni community. It is a time when families come together to prepare, participate, and celebrate their shared heritage.

Respect for the Natural World

The festival underscores the Zuni people's deep respect for the natural world. The use of feathers, turquoise, and other natural materials in the Shalako figures reflects the Zuni's close relationship with the land and its resources.

The Zuni Shalako Festival continues to be a living and essential aspect of Zuni cultural life. While it is a deeply founded tradition, it also adapts to contemporary challenges and opportunities. The festival welcomes visitors from outside the Zuni community, allowing them to witness and learn about Zuni culture and spirituality. Moreso, the Shalako Festival has become a source of cultural pride and identity for the Zuni people, reinforcing the resilience of their cultural heritage in the face of external pressures.

The Zuni Shalako Festival stands as a confirmation of the lasting strength of Zuni culture, spirituality, and community. It is a time of renewal, reflection, and celebration, marking the transition from one year to the next while honoring the Zuni ancestors, the natural world, and the lasting traditions of the Zuni people. The festival's profound significance reaches far beyond its ceremonial aspects, embodying the core values and beliefs that sustain the Zuni community and their opulent cultural heritage.

XLVIII: Seneca False Face Masks

The Seneca False Face Masks are a unique and revered cultural and spiritual tradition within the broader context of the Haudenosaunee Confederacy, also known as the Iroquois Confederacy. These distinctive carved wooden masks hold a central place in the healing ceremonies of the Seneca Nation, one of the member nations of the Haudenosaunee. The masks represent powerful and enigmatic beings known as the False Faces or Stone Coats, who are believed to possess the ability to heal, protect, and guide the Seneca people. To fully grasp the significance of the Seneca False Face Masks, one must adventure through their historical origins, symbolism, the spiritual beliefs surrounding them, their place in healing rituals, and their lasting importance within Seneca culture.

The Seneca False Face Masks have ancient foundations within Seneca culture, dating back centuries. Their origins are intertwined with Seneca mythology and the spiritual beliefs of the Seneca people. According to Seneca oral tradition, the False Faces were among the original beings created by the Creator, and they hold a unique position in Seneca cosmology. The earliest documented encounters with the Seneca False Face Masks by non-Native observers occurred in the early 17th century when European explorers and missionaries encountered the Haudenosaunee Confederacy. These encounters led to limited written records describing the masks and their use, although much of the masks' spiritual significance remained concealed from outsiders. The Seneca False Face Masks are distinctive in their appearance, characterized by their grotesque and expressive features. Each mask is carefully carved from wood, typically using white pine, and varies in size and style. The masks often display exaggerated facial features, with bulging eyes, twisted noses, and protruding tongues. These features are not meant to be frightening but rather serve as symbolic representations of the supernatural beings they embody.

The masks also incorporate elements of the natural world, like feathers, animal fur, and other materials, to enhance their spiritual potency. The use of these natural materials reflects the Seneca people's deep connection to the land and the belief that the spirits of the natural world can aid in healing. The Seneca False Face Masks are closely associated with the False Faces or Stone Coats, spiritual beings that hold immense power within Seneca cosmology. These beings are believed to possess the ability to heal illnesses, provide protection, and offer guidance to the Seneca people. The masks serve as physical vessels through which these spirits can interact with the human world.

The False Faces are respected as both benevolent and mysterious. They are believed to be capable of curing various ailments, including physical, mental, and spiritual illnesses. The Seneca people believe that when a person falls ill, it is often because the False Faces are attempting to communicate a message or provide a lesson. The masks are used in healing ceremonies to invoke the spirits and seek their guidance. The Seneca False Face Masks are central to healing rituals and ceremonies conducted by specially trained individuals known as False Face Society members or False Face Dancers. These individuals undergo rigorous training and initiation to become healers and caretakers of the masks.

Healing ceremonies involving the masks typically include the following elements:

Invocation

The False Face Society members invoke the spirits of the False Faces through prayers, songs, and chants. They don the masks and embody the spirits during the ceremony.

Dance and Performance

The False Face Dancers perform traditional dances, often in a trance-like state, while wearing the masks. These dances are believed to channel the healing energy of the spirits and aid in the healing process.

Offerings

Various offerings, like tobacco, food, and herbal medicines, are presented to the masks as gifts to the spirits. These offerings demonstrate respect and gratitude for the spirits' assistance.

Healing

The False Face Dancers approach individuals in need of healing and conduct ritualized actions, which may include blowing air, making sounds, or using special healing instruments. The goal is to help the individuals release negative energy and restore balance.

Teaching and Guidance

The False Faces are believed to impart teachings and guidance to those present during the ceremony. Their messages are often interpreted by experienced False Face Society members.

The Seneca False Face Masks continue to hold a necessary place in Seneca culture and spirituality. While traditional healing ceremonies persist, there are also efforts to preserve and revitalize the tradition for future generations. This includes the training of new False Face Society members and the documentation of oral traditions associated with the masks. Additionally, the masks have gained recognition beyond the Seneca Nation as significant works of art and cultural heritage. They are often displayed in museums and art exhibitions, allowing a wider audience to appreciate their artistic and spiritual significance.

The Seneca False Face Masks are a profound embodiment of Seneca spirituality, healing practices, and cultural heritage. They serve as a bridge between the physical and spiritual worlds, connecting the Seneca people with the benevolent and enigmatic spirits known as the False Faces. These masks continue to hold immense significance within Seneca culture, offering healing, protection, and guidance to those in need while preserving the ancient traditions and wisdom of the Seneca Nation.

XLIX: Plains Indian Sign Language

Plains Indian Sign Language (PISL), also known as Plains Sign Talk or Plains Sign Language, is an opulent and complex sign language that was historically used by indigenous peoples across the Great Plains region of North America. This unique and versatile form of communication served both practical and ceremonial purposes within Plains Indian communities. PISL allowed diverse tribes, each with their spoken languages and dialects, to communicate effectively with one another and with non-Indigenous groups like traders and settlers. To fully understand the complexity and significance of Plains Indian Sign Language, it is essential to adventure through its historical origins, its structure and vocabulary, its cultural and social roles, and its lasting heritage within Native American communities.

The origins of Plains Indian Sign Language can be traced back several centuries, long before the arrival of Europeans on the North American continent. While the precise timeline of its development remains a subject of debate among scholars, PISL likely evolved as a means of communication between indigenous groups inhabiting the giant plains of North America. The nomadic lifestyles of Plains tribes, which involved frequent mobility and interaction with neighboring tribes, created a need for a common mode of communication.

PISL also played a necessary place in trade networks among indigenous groups. Tribes engaged in extensive trade, exchanging goods like hides, food, and tools. A shared sign language facilitated negotiations and ensured mutual understanding in trade relationships.

Plains Indian Sign Language is a highly gestural and visual language that relies on a combination of hand signs, facial expressions, body movements, and contextual cues. It is important to note that PISL is not a universal sign language but rather a complex system with regional variations. Different Plains tribes developed their own dialects and variations of PISL, which allowed for nuanced communication within their specific cultural contexts. The vocabulary of PISL includes a wide range of signs that represent concepts, actions, objects, and ideas. Signers would use these signs to convey messages, engage in storytelling, negotiate trade, and participate in cultural ceremonies. Some signs are famous, meaning they visually represent the object or action they signify, while others are symbolic or abstract.

Plains Indian Sign Language played multifaceted cultural and social roles within Plains tribes:

Intertribal Communication
One of the primary functions of PISL was to facilitate communication between different Plains

tribes. This was particularly important during gatherings, trade encounters, and diplomatic meetings. PISL acted as a lingua franca, enabling tribes with distinct spoken languages to interact and cooperate effectively.

Trade and Diplomacy

Trade networks were extensive across the Great Plains, and PISL served as a means of negotiating trade agreements, exchanging information about available resources, and encouraging diplomatic relations. It helped establish trust and cooperation among tribes engaged in trade.

Cultural Transmission

PISL was used to transmit cultural knowledge, stories, and traditions from one generation to the next. It played a place in preserving the collective memory of Plains tribes, including their histories, myths, and spiritual practices.

Ceremonial and Spiritual Use

Plains Indian Sign Language was incorporated into various tribal ceremonies and rituals. Sign language was used to convey sacred messages and participate in spiritual activities. It was a means of invoking blessings, expressing gratitude, and communicating with the spiritual world.

Hunting and Warfare

PISL had practical applications in hunting and warfare. It allowed hunters and warriors to communicate silently while stalking prey or coordinating military strategies. Sign language was also employed to convey important information about the movements of game animals or enemy forces.

While Plains Indian Sign Language experienced a decline in usage with the arrival of European settlers and the imposition of Western languages, its heritage continues to persist within Native American communities. Efforts have been made to revitalize and preserve PISL as part of Native American cultural heritage. Several contemporary Native American communities and organizations are actively engaged in preserving PISL through research, education, and documentation. Language revitalization initiatives aim to pass down this unique form of communication to younger generations, ensuring that the knowledge and traditions associated with Plains Indian Sign Language endure.

Plains Indian Sign Language stands as a confirmation of the genius, adaptability, and opulent cultural heritage of Plains tribes. It served as a bridge between diverse indigenous groups, enabling them to communicate, trade, and share their cultural traditions. While the usage of PISL has diminished over time, its lasting heritage acts as a reminder of the resilience and strength of Native American cultures. Efforts to preserve and revitalize Plains Indian Sign Language are necessary in ensuring that this unique form of communication continues to be an integral part of Native American identity and heritage.

L: HOPI PROPHECIES

The Hopi people, an indigenous tribe residing in the Southwestern United States, have an opulent and profound spiritual tradition that includes a set of prophecies and insights into the future. These Hopi prophecies are deeply intertwined with their cosmology, spirituality, and cultural practices. They provide guidance on how to live in harmony with the natural world and offer wisdom for navigating the challenges of the modern world. To understand the significance of Hopi prophecies, one must dive into their historical context, the central themes and messages within these prophecies, and their relevance in today's world.

The Hopi people have inhabited the arid lands of what is now northeastern Arizona for centuries, with a history that traces back over a thousand years. Their unique cultural and spiritual traditions have been passed down through generations, and the prophecies are an integral part of their oral tradition. The Hopi prophecies are believed to have originated in the distant past, a reflection of their lasting connection to the land and the spiritual world. Hopi prophecies have been shared among the tribe's spiritual leaders, known as Katsinam or Katsinakatsina, and have been communicated through ceremonies, stories, and teachings. They offer guidance on how to maintain balance and harmony within the Hopi community and with the broader world.

The Hopi prophecies include a range of themes and messages that provide insights into their spiritual worldview and the challenges facing humanity. Some of the central themes include:

Cycles and Balance

The Hopi prophecies emphasize the importance of recognizing and respecting natural cycles. They teach that the world operates in cycles, and understanding these cycles is essential for maintaining harmony and balance in both the natural and human worlds.

Prophecies of the Four Worlds

One of the most well-known aspects of Hopi prophecies is the concept of the Four Worlds. Each world stands for a distinct era or epoch in human history. The prophecies describe how each world is characterized by specific challenges and opportunities and offer guidance on how to navigate these transitions.

The Emergence and Re-emergence

A central concept within Hopi prophecies is the idea of emergence and re-emergence. The prophecies foretell periods of upheaval and destruction, followed by opportunities for renewal and spiritual growth. The Hopi people are seen as the caretakers of the land and the knowledge needed for these transitions.

Harmony with Nature: Hopi prophecies stress the importance of living in harmony with the natural world. They teach that human actions have consequences and that respecting and caring for the land and its resources is essential for the wellness of future generations.

The True Path
Hopi prophecies guide individuals on the path of righteousness, emphasizing virtues like humility, compassion, and respect for others. They encourage individuals to live according to spiritual principles and to maintain a strong connection to the Creator.

While Hopi prophecies originated in a specific cultural and historical context, they continue to hold relevance in today's world. The teachings embedded within these prophecies offer valuable insights and guidance for addressing contemporary challenges, including environmental sustainability, social justice, and spiritual wellness.

Environmental Stewardship
Hopi prophecies emphasize the importance of living in harmony with nature. In an era marked by environmental degradation and climate change, these teachings encourage responsible stewardship of the Earth and its resources.

Cultural Preservation

Hopi prophecies hold a necessary place in preserving and revitalizing Hopi culture and traditions. They serve as a source of cultural identity and continuity for the Hopi people, reminding them of their sacred responsibilities.

Spiritual Guidance

The moral and ethical teachings within Hopi prophecies offer valuable insights into living a meaningful and purposeful life. They inspire individuals to seek spiritual growth and to recognize their enmeshment with all of creation.

Intertribal and Global Relevance

While Hopi prophecies are specific to the Hopi people, their messages of balance, respect for nature, and spiritual principles vibe with indigenous communities worldwide. They serve as a reminder of the shared values and wisdom found among indigenous cultures globally.

In summary, Hopi prophecies are a profound and lasting aspect of Hopi culture and spirituality. They offer insights into the cyclical nature of existence, the importance of balance and harmony, and the path to righteousness. In today's world, these prophecies continue to hold relevance by guiding individuals and communities toward a more sustainable, just, and spiritually connected future. They remind us of the lasting wisdom found within indigenous traditions and the importance of respecting and learning from these cultural treasures.

LI: MUSCOGEE STOMP DANCE

The Muscogee (Creek) Stomp Dance, known as "Hutkke" in the Muscogee language, is a living and deeply spiritual ceremonial dance at the heart of Muscogee (Creek) culture. This ancient tradition holds immense significance for the Muscogee people, one of the indigenous nations of the Southeastern United States. The Stomp Dance is not merely a form of entertainment but a sacred ritual that connects participants to their ancestors, the natural world, and the Creator. To understand the profound cultural and spiritual importance of the Muscogee Stomp Dance, one must adventure through its historical foundations, the structure and symbolism of the dance, its place within Muscogee society, and its continued vitality in contemporary times.

The Muscogee (Creek) Nation has a long and complex history that predates European contact. Their ancestors, known as the Mississippian culture, built elaborate mound structures and developed sophisticated agricultural practices in the Southeastern United States, including present-day Alabama, Georgia, and Florida. The Stomp Dance traces its origins to these ancient traditions. When European settlers arrived in the Southeast, they encountered the Muscogee people, who had established a network of towns and villages along rivers and fertile lands. The Stomp Dance was already a central element of Muscogee society, and it continued to thrive despite the challenges posed by colonialism.

The Muscogee Stomp Dance is a complex and multi-faceted ceremonial event. It is typically held in a square or circular open-air arbor called a "stomp ground" or "dance ground." The dance is characterized by the rhythmic beat of a large drum, which is played by a group of men known as the "Hutkemalgeta" or "Drummers."

Key elements of the Stomp Dance include

Dance Styles

The Stomp Dance incorporates various dance styles, including the "Closed Dance" and the "Open Dance." Participants, known as "Stomp Dancers," are divided into men and women, each with specific roles and steps.

Drumming and Singing

The Drummers sing songs in the Muscogee language, accompanied by the beat of the drum. These songs are traditional and carry deep cultural and spiritual significance. The rhythm of the drum and the cadence of the songs guide the movements of the dancers.

Fire

A central fire burns at the center of the dance ground. It is tended throughout the night and symbolizes the hearth and the presence of the Creator.

Regalia

Stomp Dancers wear distinctive regalia, which includes brightly colored clothing adorned with traditional designs, shell shakers on their legs, and feathers or fans in their hands. The regalia reflects the individual's connection to their clan and their place in the dance.

Turtle Shell Shakers

Men and women wear turtle shell shakers on their legs. These shakers produce a distinctive rhythmic sound as they dance, contributing to the overall music of the ceremony.

The Muscogee Stomp Dance holds a central place within Muscogee society, encompassing various roles and functions:

Spiritual Connection

The Stomp Dance is a profound spiritual experience that connects participants to their ancestors, the natural world, and the Creator. It is a time for prayer, reflection, and seeking guidance.

Community and Identity

The dance acts as a unifying force within the Muscogee community, reinforcing a sense of shared identity and cultural continuity. It brings families and clans together, strengthening social bonds.

Healing and Blessings

The Stomp Dance is often used for healing purposes, with prayers offered for the wellness of individuals facing illness or challenges. It is also a time for giving thanks and seeking blessings for the community.

Cultural Preservation

The Stomp Dance plays an important place in preserving Muscogee cultural traditions, language, and songs. It is a living expression of Muscogee identity and heritage.

The Muscogee Stomp Dance remains a living and thriving tradition within Muscogee culture. While it has faced challenges over the centuries, including efforts to suppress indigenous practices, it has endured and adapted to changing circumstances. Today, the Stomp Dance continues to be performed in Muscogee communities both within and beyond Oklahoma, where many Muscogee people were forcibly relocated during the 19th century. Efforts to revitalize and pass down the Stomp Dance to younger generations are ongoing. Muscogee elders and cultural leaders hold an important place in teaching the dance and its associated customs to ensure its continued vitality.

In closing, the Muscogee (Creek) Stomp Dance is a profound and lasting expression of Muscogee culture, spirituality, and identity. It stands as a confirmation of the resilience of indigenous traditions in the face of historical challenges. As a sacred and communal event, it continues to enrich the lives of Muscogee people and acts as a source of pride, cultural preservation, and spiritual connection with their ancestors and the Creator.

LII: navajo night chant

The Navajo Night Chant, also known as "Tłʼééjí" or "Nightway," is a profound and complex healing ceremony deeply founded in Navajo culture and spirituality. This sacred ritual, which takes place over several nights, is aimed at restoring balance and harmony to individuals who are suffering from physical, emotional, or spiritual ailments. The Night Chant is characterized by its elaborate sandpaintings, powerful chants, prayers, and the involvement of skilled medicine men, known as "Hataałii," who serve as the ceremonial leaders. To fully appreciate the significance of the Navajo Night Chant, one must adventure through its historical origins, its structure and components, the symbolism within its rituals, and its place in contemporary Navajo society.

The Navajo people, also known as the Diné, have an opulent history that extends back centuries in the Southwestern United States. The Night Chant is believed to have originated in the distant past, with its exact origins shrouded in the mists of time. It is respected as one of the most important and revered ceremonies within Navajo culture. The Navajo Night Chant has been passed down through generations within specific Navajo clans, each responsible for preserving and conducting the ceremony. It reflects the Diné worldview, which centers on the principles of balance, harmony, and enmeshment with the natural and spiritual worlds.

The Night Chant is a carefully structured healing ceremony, and its components are carried out with great precision and attention to detail. It typically unfolds over a series of nights, with each night committed to specific rituals and purposes. Key elements of the Night Chant include:

Sandpaintings

Central to the Night Chant are the complex sandpaintings, known as "iikaah," created by the Hataałii. These sandpaintings are complex, temporary works of art, painstakingly crafted on the floor of the hogan, a traditional Navajo dwelling. They feature symbolic images and designs representing various aspects of the ceremony, including deities, sacred mountains, and healing motifs. The act of creating these sandpaintings is respected as a sacred act in itself.

Chants and Songs

The Night Chant is accompanied by a series of chants and songs, known as "kéji." These chants are performed by the Hataałii and serve multiple purposes, including invoking the deities, guiding the healing process, and maintaining the spiritual focus of the ceremony. The songs are passed down orally and are specific to the Night Chant.

Prayers and Offerings

Throughout the ceremony, prayers are offered to seek blessings, healing, and protection. Offerings of corn pollen, tobacco, and other symbolic items are made as part of the prayer rituals.

Sweat Bath

Participants in the Night Chant may undergo a sweat bath as a form of purification before the ceremony. This practice involves entering a small, enclosed space with heated stones to induce sweating and cleanse the body.

Dance and Movement

The Hataałii and participants engage in specific dances and movements as part of the ceremony. These movements are coordinated with the chants, songs, and sandpaintings, enhancing the overall spiritual experience.

The symbolism within the Night Chant is multi-layered and carries deep cultural and spiritual significance:

Healing

The primary purpose of the Night Chant is healing. It is believed that illness, both physical and spiritual, is often the result of disharmony or imbalance. The sandpaintings, chants, and rituals are designed to restore this balance and promote healing.

Connection to Deities

The deities invoked in the Night Chant hold a central place in guiding the healing process. Each sandpainting stands for a specific deity, and the chants are a means of communication with these spiritual beings.

Enmeshment

The Night Chant focuses on the enmeshment of all living beings, the natural world, and the spiritual world. It reaffirms the Navajo belief that harmony with one's surroundings is essential for wellness.

Cultural Preservation

The Night Chant is a living embodiment of Navajo culture and spirituality. It acts as a repository of traditional knowledge and practices, ensuring their continuation for future generations.

Despite the challenges posed by modernity, the Navajo Night Chant continues to be a necessary and living part of Navajo culture. While the ceremony may have evolved to accommodate contemporary contexts, its core principles and spiritual significance remain intact. The Night Chant is still performed to address various forms of illness and to maintain the spiritual and cultural identity of the Navajo people. Efforts are made to pass down the knowledge and skills required to conduct the Night Chant to the next generation of Hataałii, ensuring the continuity of this sacred tradition. It also underscores the resilience of Navajo culture in preserving and adapting its spiritual practices to address the evolving needs of its community.

The Navajo Night Chant stands as a confirmation of the depth and complexity of Navajo culture and spirituality. It is a ceremony of profound healing, spiritual connection, and cultural preservation. Through its complex rituals, sandpaintings, chants, and prayers, the Night Chant offers insight into the Navajo worldview, emphasizing the lasting importance of balance, harmony, and enmeshment in the face of life's challenges.

LIII: Lakota Four Directions Teaching

The Lakota people, among other indigenous tribes of North America, have a deep and spiritual connection to the natural world, including the cardinal directions: North, East, South, and West. The concept of the Four Directions holds profound significance in Lakota belief, encompassing not just physical orientation but also spiritual and cultural elements. To understand the spiritual richness of the Lakota Four Directions Teaching, one must adventure through its historical foundations, its symbolism, its place in daily life and ceremonies, and its lasting relevance in Lakota culture today. The Lakota, also known as the Sioux, are a Plains Indian tribe with an opulent history that spans thousands of years. Their spiritual traditions, including the reverence for the Four Directions, have been passed down through generations. The Four Directions Teaching is deeply intertwined with the Lakota worldview, reflecting their profound connection to the land, the seasons, and the cosmos.

In Lakota belief, each of the four cardinal directions carries unique symbolism and significance:

North (WiiyayA)

The North is associated with the cold season, winter, and the color white. It stands for wisdom, introspection, and the elders. It is a time for reflection and gaining knowledge from the past.

East (Wíiyela)

The East is linked to the rising sun, new beginnings, and the color red. It symbolizes youth, growth, and renewal. It is a direction associated with birth and the emergence of life.

South (Wíiyohi:)

The South is connected to the warmth of summer, the color yellow, and abundance. It stands for the time of growth, maturation, and the fullness of life. It is a direction associated with action and vitality.

West (WiiyangA)

The West is linked to the setting sun, the color black, and introspection. It stands for the time of decline, maturity, and the transition to the spirit world. It is a direction associated with the ancestors and the afterlife.

The Lakota Four Directions Teaching is not limited to the abstract world of symbolism; it is deeply integrated into daily life, ceremonies, and rituals:

Sundance Ceremony

The Sundance, one of the most important Lakota ceremonies, involves the construction of a sacred arbor aligned with the Four Directions. Participants fast, dance, and pray facing each direction, seeking guidance, and spiritual renewal.

Vision Quest

Young Lakota individuals begin on vision quests, which typically involve spending time alone in nature, fasting, and seeking visions. The Four Directions hold an important place in guiding the vision quester and interpreting their experiences.

Smudging

The burning of sacred herbs, like sage or sweetgrass, is a common practice among the Lakota for purification and spiritual cleansing. The smoke is often directed to each of the Four Directions to purify and bless a space or individual.

Naming Ceremonies

When a child is born, their name is often chosen with consideration of the Four Directions. The direction associated with the child's birth or other significant factors may influence their name.

Daily Prayers and Blessings

Many Lakota individuals begin their day with prayers and offerings made to the Four Directions. This practice seeks guidance, protection, and a harmonious start to the day.

The Lakota Four Directions Teaching remains a living and lasting aspect of Lakota culture and spirituality. While contemporary life has introduced new challenges and influences, the

Lakota people continue to uphold these traditions as a means of connecting with their heritage and maintaining their spiritual wellness. In the face of cultural preservation efforts and the transmission of traditional knowledge to younger generations, the Four Directions Teaching continues to serve as a foundational element of Lakota identity and spirituality. It reminds the Lakota people of their connection to the land, their ancestors, and the cycles of nature, encouraging a sense of balance and harmony in their lives.

The Lakota Four Directions Teaching is a profound and multi-faceted aspect of Lakota culture and spirituality. It includes an opulent atlas of symbolism, daily practices, and ceremonial rituals that reflect the Lakota worldview and their deep connection to the natural world. The Four Directions serve as a compass guiding the Lakota people in their adventure through life, connecting them to the past, the present, and the future, and reinforcing the lasting importance of balance and harmony in their way of life.

LIV: NEZ PERCE LONGHOUSE RELIGION

The Nez Perce Longhouse Religion, also known as the Washani or Seven Drums Religion, is a unique spiritual movement that emerged among the Nez Perce tribe in the late 19th century. It stands for a blend of Christian and traditional indigenous beliefs, creating a syncretic and culturally significant religious system. To understand the Nez Perce Longhouse Religion, one must adventure through its historical context, its core beliefs and practices, its place in Nez Perce society, and its ongoing significance today.

The Nez Perce, also known as the Nimiipuu, are an indigenous people who traditionally inhabited the Pacific Northwest, including parts of present-day Idaho, Oregon, Washington, and Montana. Their culture and spirituality were deeply founded in the natural world, with an emphasis on the relationship between humans and the land. The emergence of the Nez Perce Longhouse Religion can be traced to the late 19th century, a time of profound change and upheaval for indigenous peoples across North America. The arrival of Euro-American settlers, the encroachment on Nez Perce lands, and the imposition of Christianity were significant factors in the development of this syncretic religious movement.

The Nez Perce Longhouse Religion incorporates elements of both Christianity and traditional Nez Perce spirituality. Key beliefs and practices include:

Monotheism
The Longhouse Religion centers on the belief in a single, supreme deity often referred to as "God" or "the Creator." This monotheistic concept aligns with certain Christian teachings.

Christian Influence
The Longhouse Religion incorporates Christian elements like the Bible, hymns, and Christian symbols. It embraces aspects of Christianity, like the belief in Jesus Christ as a spiritual figure.

Sweat Lodge Ceremonies
Traditional Nez Perce sweat lodge ceremonies are an integral part of the Longhouse Religion. These ceremonies involve purification through steam and prayer and are conducted in sweat lodges made of saplings and covered with blankets or hides.

Seven Drums
The Longhouse Religion derives its name from the use of seven drums, each representing a specific spiritual teaching or prophecy. These drums are central to the religious ceremonies and rituals.

Prophecy and Visionary Experiences

The Longhouse Religion places a strong emphasis on prophecy and visionary experiences. Spiritual leaders receive visions that guide the community and provide insight into the spiritual world.

Dances and Rituals

The religion includes various dances and rituals performed during religious gatherings and ceremonies. These dances are accompanied by singing and drumming and serve to connect participants with the Creator.

The Nez Perce Longhouse Religion played a significant place in Nez Perce society during a time of immense cultural change and upheaval. It served several important functions:

Cultural Resilience

The Longhouse Religion provided a means for the Nez Perce to maintain their cultural identity and traditional practices in the face of external pressures to assimilate into Euro-American ways of life.

Spiritual Guidance

The religion offered spiritual guidance and a sense of purpose during a period of profound cultural disruption. It provided a scaffolding for understanding and coping with the challenges posed by colonization and loss of ancestral lands.

Community Cohesion

The Longhouse Religion encouraged a sense of community and unity among the Nez Perce. It provided a space for collective worship, prayer, and the sharing of spiritual experiences.

Resistance and Adaptation

Some Nez Perce leaders who practiced the Longhouse Religion played prominent roles in the Nez Perce War of 1877, resisting forced relocation and land dispossession. After the war, the religion continued to evolve and adapt to changing circumstances.

The Nez Perce Longhouse Religion continues to hold cultural and spiritual significance for the Nez Perce people today. While it has evolved over time and faced challenges, it remains an essential part of Nez Perce identity and heritage. Efforts are made to pass down the teachings and practices of the religion to younger generations, ensuring its continuation. In recent years, there has been a resurgence of interest in traditional Nez Perce spirituality, including the Longhouse Religion. This revival reflects a broader movement among indigenous communities to reconnect with their ancestral beliefs and practices and to preserve their cultural heritage.

In closing, the Nez Perce Longhouse Religion stands for a unique blend of Christian and indigenous spirituality that emerged in response to the challenges faced by the Nez Perce people during the late 19th century. It acts as a confirmation of the resilience and adaptability of indigenous spiritual traditions in the face of cultural change and external pressures. Today, it continues to be a source of cultural identity, spiritual guidance, and community cohesion among the Nez Perce, reinforcing the lasting importance of indigenous spirituality in the contemporary world.

LV: Anishinaabe Seven Fires Prophecy

The Anishinaabe Seven Fires Prophecy is a sacred and prophetic teaching central to Anishinaabe (Ojibwe, Odawa, Potawatomi) spirituality and worldview. Passed down through oral tradition for generations, the prophecy consists of a series of seven visions that foretell the spiritual, cultural, and environmental challenges and opportunities that the Anishinaabe people would face in their adventure through time. To fully appreciate the significance of the Seven Fires Prophecy, it is essential to dive into its historical origins, its interpretations and teachings, its relevance in contemporary Anishinaabe communities, and its broader implications for all of humanity. The Anishinaabe, whose name means "Original People" or "First People," are indigenous to the Great Lakes region and parts of the surrounding areas in North America. The Seven Fires Prophecy is believed to have originated among the Anishinaabe people, particularly among the Ojibwe, whose homeland extends across the Great Lakes region into the northern Midwest and Canada.

The origins of the prophecy are shrouded in the mists of time, reflecting the ancient spiritual traditions and deep connection the Anishinaabe have with their ancestral lands. It is said to have been revealed to spiritual leaders and visionaries during periods of reflection and prayer.

The Seven Fires Prophecy consists of seven distinct visions, each with its own unique message.

While interpretations may vary among Anishinaabe communities and individuals, the following is a general overview of the core teachings and themes associated with each of the seven fires:

First Fire (Wiigwaasabak)

The first vision speaks of a time when the Anishinaabe people were living in their homeland along the eastern coast of North America. It is a time of spiritual and cultural purity, symbolized by the sacred birch bark scrolls (wiigwaasabak) that contain their teachings.

Second Fire (Nibiishabak)

The second vision marks a period of migration westward in search of a "food that grows upon the water." This vision reflects the Anishinaabe's adventure to the Great Lakes region and their relationship with wild rice (manoomin), a staple food source.

Third Fire (Ogichi-taadine)

The third vision depicts a time of conflict and division among the Anishinaabe, symbolized by the arrival of the "Iron Boats" or European colonizers. This period stands for a challenge to the Anishinaabe way of life and a need for unity.

Fourth Fire (Nika-taadine)

The fourth vision foretells a time of great hardship, marked by disease, ecological imbalance, and societal disruption. It acts as a warning of the consequences of straying from traditional teachings and values.

Fifth Fire (Nizo-taadine)

The fifth vision speaks of a period of rebirth and cultural resurgence. The Anishinaabe are told that they will face a choice: to follow the path of the Fourth Fire's destruction or to get in touch with the traditional teachings and rekindle the Anishinaabe spirit.

Sixth Fire (Noondaagotaabini)

The sixth vision describes a time when the Anishinaabe will be offered a choice between two paths, one materialistic and destructive and the other spiritual and harmonious with the natural world. The choice they make will determine their fate and the fate of all living beings.

Seventh Fire (Akii-inabek)

The seventh and final vision speaks of a time when the Anishinaabe people, having chosen the right path, will come together with other indigenous and non-indigenous peoples to heal the earth and restore balance. It is a time of universal peace and unity.

The Seven Fires Prophecy continues to hold deep spiritual and cultural significance within Anishinaabe communities today. It acts as a guiding scaffolding for understanding the challenges and opportunities facing the Anishinaabe people in the modern world. Efforts are made to pass down the teachings of the prophecy to younger generations, ensuring its continuity and relevance.

In contemporary Anishinaabe communities, the prophecy is viewed as a call to action, emphasizing the importance of reconnecting with traditional values, restoring harmony with the natural world, and encouraging unity among all people. It is also seen as a source of hope and resilience, reminding the Anishinaabe people of their lasting spiritual strength.

While the Seven Fires Prophecy is deeply founded in Anishinaabe culture, its teachings have broader implications for all of humanity. Its message of unity, spiritual renewal, and environmental stewardship vibes with people from diverse backgrounds who are concerned about the wellness of the planet and the need for a more harmonious way of living.

In an era marked by environmental challenges, social divisions, and cultural disconnection, the teachings of the Seven Fires Prophecy offer valuable insights into the path toward healing and renewal. It invites individuals and communities to reflect on their choices and their effect on the world, emphasizing the importance of choosing a path that leads to greater harmony, respect, and unity among all living beings.

The Anishinaabe Seven Fires Prophecy is a profound and spiritually opulent teaching that continues to guide the Anishinaabe people and inspire others who seek a deeper connection to the natural world and a more harmonious way of living. It reminds one of the lasting wisdom of indigenous cultures and their vision for a future in which all people come together to heal the earth and restore balance to our world.

LVI: NORTHWEST COAST TOTEM POLES

Northwest Coast Totem Poles, magnificent and intricately carved sculptures, stand as famous symbols of the indigenous peoples of the Pacific Northwest, particularly among the tribes of the Haida, Tlingit, Coast Salish, Kwakwaka'wakw, and Nuu-chah-nulth. These imposing wooden structures, often reaching towering heights, serve multifaceted purposes in the opulent cultural and spiritual atlas of the Northwest Coast First Nations. To fully appreciate the significance of Northwest Coast Totem Poles, one must dive into their historical origins, their artistic and symbolic elements, their place in indigenous society, and their contemporary relevance.

The tradition of carving totem poles among the indigenous peoples of the Pacific Northwest Coast has deep historical foundations dating back centuries. These monumental wooden sculptures have their origins in the ancestral traditions of these diverse and culturally opulent societies. Totem poles were traditionally created using cedar, a sacred tree with spiritual significance, and each carving conveyed stories, genealogies, and cultural beliefs. The history of totem pole carving is closely intertwined with oral traditions, and these sculptures served as a tangible record of indigenous histories and legacies. Totem poles are renowned for their exquisite craftsmanship and complex detailing. They are characterized by a variety of artistic elements and symbols, each of which holds profound cultural and spiritual significance:

Animals

Animal figures, like bears, eagles, wolves, and ravens, are commonly described on totem poles. Each animal stands for different qualities, characteristics, or clan affiliations within indigenous communities.

Human Figures

Human figures on totem poles may represent ancestors, important historical figures, or mythological beings. These figures often wear traditional regalia and convey specific stories or teachings.

Crests

Crests are family or clan symbols that are passed down through generations. Totem poles may display crests that identify the lineage and history of a particular family or group.

Color

Totem poles are traditionally painted in living colors using natural pigments. Each color has its own significance, like red symbolizing life and black representing the spirit world.

Positioning

The placement of figures on a totem pole is deliberate and meaningful. Figures are often stacked vertically, with the most important or powerful figures placed at the top.

Formlines

Totem pole designs are structured using formlines, a distinctive artistic style characterized by curvilinear shapes and geometric patterns. Formlines are an essential part of Northwest Coast art.

Totem poles serve a multitude of roles in indigenous society, encompassing cultural, spiritual, and social functions:

Narrative Art

Totem poles are narrative art forms that tell stories, recount historical events, and convey cultural teachings. They function as visual representations of oral traditions, preserving indigenous knowledge and histories.

Community and Clan Identity

Totem poles are a source of pride and identity for indigenous communities. They often depict clan crests and serve as markers of territorial ownership and affiliation.

Spiritual Significance

Totem poles have spiritual significance and are often raised during potlatch ceremonies, feasts, and other important gatherings. They connect the living with the spirit world and ancestors.

Educational Tools

Totem poles are educational tools used to transmit cultural knowledge and values to younger generations. They help teach indigenous youth about their heritage and traditions.

Tourism and Cultural Expression

In contemporary times, totem poles also hold a place in cultural expression and tourism. They are displayed in museums, parks, and public spaces, allowing a broader audience to appreciate and learn from their beauty and cultural significance.

Totem poles continue to hold great significance in the lives of indigenous peoples of the Pacific Northwest. They are not relics of the past but living symbols of resilience and cultural revival. In recent years, there has been a resurgence in totem pole carving, with skilled artists and carvers working to preserve and revitalize this ancient art form. Totem poles also hold a place in contemporary indigenous activism and cultural revitalization efforts. They are used to assert indigenous land rights, highlight environmental issues, and promote cultural awareness and pride. Additionally, totem poles serve as a bridge between generations, ensuring that traditional knowledge and artistic techniques are passed on to younger indigenous artists and community members.

Northwest Coast Totem Poles are remarkable expressions of indigenous art, culture, and spirituality. They stand as powerful symbols of the opulent traditions and lasting legacies of the indigenous peoples of the Pacific Northwest Coast. These majestic wooden sculptures continue to inspire awe and admiration while serving as a confirmation of the resilience and cultural vitality of indigenous communities, both in the past and in the present.

LVII: ALGONQUIN BIRCH BARK SCROLLS

The Algonquin Birch Bark Scrolls, also known as Wiigwaasabak (singular: Wiigwaasabak), are sacred and ancient manuscripts created by the Algonquin people, a group of indigenous cultures living in the northeastern woodlands of North America. These scrolls are made from the inner bark of the paper birch tree (Betula papyrifera) and serve as repositories of ceremonial knowledge, songs, stories, and spiritual teachings. To fully appreciate the significance of the Algonquin Birch Bark Scrolls, one must adventure through their historical origins, their complex artistic features, their place in Algonquin culture, and their contemporary importance in preserving indigenous heritage.

The tradition of creating birch bark scrolls has deep historical foundations among the Algonquin and other indigenous cultures of the northeastern woodlands. These scrolls are believed to have been in use for centuries, passed down through generations of knowledge keepers, spiritual leaders, and storytellers. The paper birch tree, a prominent species in the region, provides the raw material for the scrolls. Its inner bark is harvested in a sustainable manner, and the resulting material is carefully prepared for use as writing material.

Algonquin Birch Bark Scrolls are renowned for their artistic and aesthetic qualities. They exhibit several distinctive features:

Birch Bark Medium

The scrolls are made from the inner bark of the paper birch tree, which is both durable and pliable. This material can be folded, rolled, or sewn together to create scroll-like manuscripts.

Pictographs

Algonquin scrolls often feature pictographs or painted symbols that convey meaning and context. These symbols are used to represent animals, plants, celestial bodies, and other elements of the natural and spiritual worlds.

Text and Images

Scrolls may include both text and images, creating a visual narrative. Text is often written using charcoal, graphite, or other natural pigments.

Ornate Borders

Many scrolls feature ornate borders and decorative motifs, reflecting the aesthetic sensibilities of Algonquin artisans.

Sewn Bindings

Sections of birch bark are sewn together using materials like plant fibers or sinew to create longer scrolls.

Rolled or Folded Format

Scrolls can be rolled up or folded for storage and transport, making them portable and convenient for use in ceremonies and teachings.

The Algonquin Birch Bark Scrolls hold several important roles within Algonquin culture and spirituality:

Ceremonial Record Keeping

These scrolls serve as repositories of ceremonial knowledge, documenting the rituals, songs, and prayers used in important ceremonies. They are consulted by spiritual leaders and participants to ensure the correct performance of ceremonies.

Oral Tradition Preservation

Algonquin scrolls are instrumental in preserving the oral tradition of the Algonquin people. They contain stories, myths, and histories passed down through generations, ensuring that these cultural narratives endure.

Spiritual Guidance

Spiritual leaders and knowledge keepers refer to the scrolls to gain insights into traditional Algonquin spirituality. They offer guidance on connecting with the spiritual world and maintaining balance and harmony.

Teaching and Education
Birch bark scrolls are used as educational tools to impart traditional knowledge to younger generations. They are a means of passing down cultural heritage, language, and spiritual teachings.

Medicinal and Herbal Knowledge
Some scrolls contain information about the medicinal uses of plants, herbs, and natural remedies, reflecting the deep connection between nature and indigenous healing practices.

The Algonquin Birch Bark Scrolls continue to hold immense cultural and spiritual significance in contemporary Algonquin communities. They are seen as repositories of ancestral wisdom and cultural identity, helping to revitalize and preserve Algonquin heritage. Several factors contribute to their ongoing importance:

Cultural Revival
Algonquin communities are actively engaged in cultural revitalization efforts, and the scrolls hold a necessary place in this process. They are used in cultural workshops, language programs, and educational initiatives to pass down traditional knowledge.

Language Revitalization

The scrolls contain texts in the Algonquin language, making them valuable resources in language revitalization efforts. Language preservation is a key component of maintaining cultural identity.

Spiritual Continuity

The scrolls serve as a bridge between generations, allowing spiritual leaders and knowledge keepers to mentor younger community members in the practice of traditional ceremonies and spiritual beliefs.

Collaboration with Researchers

Indigenous scholars and researchers collaborate with academic institutions to study and document the scrolls, ensuring that they are preserved for future generations.

In conclusion, the Algonquin Birch Bark Scrolls are priceless cultural treasures that provide insights into the history, spirituality, and traditions of the Algonquin people. They continue to serve as necessary conduits for the transmission of knowledge, ensuring that the opulent cultural heritage of the Algonquin people endures and thrives in the contemporary world. These scrolls stand as a confirmation of the resilience and cultural vitality of indigenous communities and their lasting

commitment to preserving their heritage for generations to come.

LVIII: PAIUTE CIRCLE DANCE

The Paiute Circle Dance, also known as the Ghost Dance, holds a significant place in the history and spirituality of Native American communities, particularly among the Paiute and other Plains and Western tribes. This dance emerged in the late 19th century as part of a pan-Indian spiritual movement that prophesized a rebirth of Native American cultures and the restoration of their ancestral lands. To fully understand the Paiute Circle Dance, one must adventure through its historical origins, its core teachings and rituals, its place in Native American resistance and revitalization, and its lasting heritage in indigenous communities.

The foundations of the Paiute Circle Dance can be traced back to the teachings of Wovoka, a Paiute prophet also known as Jack Wilson. Wovoka received a series of visions in the late 19th century that formed the basis of the Ghost Dance movement. He prophesized that Native Americans should participate in a spiritual dance, the Ghost Dance, which would not just bring about a renewal of indigenous traditions but also lead to a time of peace, unity, and the return of ancestral lands. Wovoka's teachings spread rapidly among various tribes in the Plains and Western regions of North America. The Ghost Dance became a unifying force among indigenous peoples who had endured displacement, violence, and cultural suppression as a result of European colonization.

The Paiute Circle Dance, or Ghost Dance, is characterized by a set of core teachings and rituals that were central to its practice:

Circle Dance

Participants would form a large circle and dance counterclockwise, symbolizing the turning back of time and the return of ancestors. The dance was accompanied by singing, drumming, and chanting.

Regalia

Dancers wore special regalia that often included white or ghostly-colored garments. These symbolic outfits represented purity and spiritual transformation.

Prayer and Meditation

The Ghost Dance involved deep spiritual elements, with participants engaging in prayer and meditation during the dance. They searched out to connect with the spirit world and receive guidance from ancestors.

Prophecies

The Ghost Dance incorporated various prophecies, including the belief that the Earth would shake and reshape itself to return ancestral lands to Native peoples. It also prophesized the end of suffering and the restoration of traditional ways of life.

Nonviolence

A key element of the Ghost Dance movement was its commitment to nonviolence. It emphasized peaceful coexistence and unity among tribes, with the hope that these qualities would lead to positive change.

The Paiute Circle Dance, or Ghost Dance, played a necessary place in Native American resistance and cultural revitalization during a tumultuous period in their history:

Cultural Revival

The Ghost Dance movement provided a platform for the revival of indigenous cultural practices, languages, and spirituality. It offered a sense of hope and unity during a time of great adversity.

Resistance to Assimilation

Indigenous peoples had endured forced assimilation, displacement, and violence for decades. The Ghost Dance represented a spiritual and cultural resistance against these oppressive forces.

Unity Among Tribes

The movement united diverse Native American tribes in a shared vision of renewal and restoration. It transcended tribal bounds and encouraged a sense of solidarity among indigenous communities.

Government Response

The U.S. government, alarmed by the growing popularity of the Ghost Dance, viewed it as a potential threat and responded with repression. This led to the tragic Wounded Knee Massacre in 1890, where hundreds of Lakota Sioux were killed.

Continued Significance

While the Ghost Dance movement did not achieve all of its prophesized outcomes, it left an undying mark on Native American history. It continues to be remembered and honored in contemporary indigenous ceremonies and cultural practices.

The heritage of the Paiute Circle Dance, or Ghost Dance, endures in modern indigenous communities:

Spiritual Continuity

The Ghost Dance remains a part of indigenous spiritual practices, with some communities incorporating its teachings into their ceremonies and dances.

Cultural Identity

The movement's emphasis on cultural revitalization and unity remains a source of encouragement for indigenous peoples seeking to preserve their languages, traditions, and ways of life.

Resilience

The history of the Ghost Dance acts as a confirmation of the resilience of Native American communities in the face of adversity. It reminds indigenous peoples of their lasting spiritual strength and cultural heritage.

Historical Awareness

The Ghost Dance movement is an important part of Native American history, and it is studied and remembered as a significant chapter in the struggle for indigenous rights and cultural preservation.

The Paiute Circle Dance, or Ghost Dance, holds a prominent place in the history and spirituality of Native American communities. It emerged as a response to centuries of colonization, displacement, and cultural suppression, offering hope, unity, and a vision of cultural revival. While it faced repression and tragedy, its teachings and heritage continue to inspire indigenous peoples in their ongoing adventure to preserve their cultural heritage and spiritual traditions.

LIX: UTE BEAR DANCE

The Ute Bear Dance, deeply founded in Ute mythology and culture, is a springtime ceremonial dance of profound significance among the Ute people, who are indigenous to the Great Basin and the Rocky Mountain regions of North America. This dance, known as the "Thigwap" or "Thi'kara" in the Ute language, is not just a celebration of the arrival of spring but also a spiritual ceremony that connects the Ute people with their ancestral traditions, the natural world, and the sacred bear. To comprehensively adventure through the Ute Bear Dance, it is essential to dive into its historical origins, the symbolism of the bear, the rituals and practices associated with the dance, and its contemporary significance within the Ute community. The Ute Bear Dance has ancient foundations that can be traced back for generations within Ute culture. It is believed to have been practiced for centuries, serving as a necessary tradition that reinforces the Ute people's deep connection to the land, the seasons, and their spiritual beliefs. The dance has its origins in Ute mythology, which tells the story of the bear's place as a messenger between the Ute people and the spirit world.

According to Ute legend, the bear, known as "Hohnok" or "Thigwap" in their language, played a significant place in facilitating communication between the living and the spirit world. It is said that the bear would enter the spirit world during hibernation and return in the spring to deliver messages and blessings to the Ute people. The Bear Dance, therefore, symbolizes the awakening of the bear from hibernation and the renewal of this spiritual connection.

The bear holds profound symbolism in Ute culture and the Bear Dance itself:

Messenger of the Spirit World

The bear is seen as a mediator between the Ute people and the spirits of the land. Its emergence from hibernation stands for the return of spiritual guidance and blessings.

Springtime and Renewal

The bear's awakening from hibernation aligns with the arrival of spring, symbolizing the renewal of life, the natural world, and Ute traditions.

Strength and Resilience

Bears are admired for their strength and resilience, qualities that the Ute people have historically embodied in their daily lives.

Spiritual Protector

The bear is regarded as a spiritual protector, ensuring the wellness of the Ute people and their connection to the land.

The Ute Bear Dance is a multifaceted ceremonial event that involves various rituals and practices:

Preparation

Preparation for the dance begins long before the actual event. Ute families and communities gather to make complex bear dance regalia, which includes clothing adorned with bear claws, bear fur, and other symbolic elements. This regalia is worn by the dancers during the ceremony.

Dance Ground

A specific dance ground is prepared for the event, often in a natural outdoor setting. The dance ground is respected as sacred, and its location is chosen with care.

Dancing and Singing

The Bear Dance involves group dancing and singing. Dancers form circles and move in a counterclockwise direction, symbolizing the bear's awakening from hibernation. Singers and drummers provide the rhythmic accompaniment to the dance, singing traditional Bear Dance songs.

Offerings and Prayer

The ceremony includes offerings to the bear and prayers for blessings, protection, and renewal.

These offerings typically include food, tobacco, and other symbolic items.

Interactions with the Bear
In some variations of the dance, a bear effigy or representation may be present, symbolizing the bear's place as a messenger between worlds.

Community and Sharing
The Bear Dance is a communal event that encourages unity and sharing within the Ute community. It provides an opportunity for social interaction, the passing down of traditions, and the strengthening of cultural ties.

The Ute Bear Dance remains a living and meaningful tradition within the Ute community, serving several contemporary purposes:

Cultural Preservation
The dance plays an important place in preserving Ute culture, language, and traditions. It provides a link to the past and ensures that ancestral knowledge is passed down to younger generations.

Spiritual Connection
The Bear Dance maintains the spiritual connection between the Ute people, the natural world, and their ancestors. It reinforces the belief in the bear as a messenger of the spirit world.

Community Bonding

The Bear Dance strengthens community bonds and encourages a sense of belonging and identity among the Ute people. It is a time for celebration, sharing, and collective reflection.

Educational Tool

The Bear Dance acts as an educational tool, helping to teach younger generations about Ute mythology, traditions, and the importance of environmental stewardship.

Cultural Revitalization

In recent years, there has been a resurgence of interest in the Bear Dance among Ute communities. Efforts to revitalize and perpetuate this tradition have led to its continued practice and relevance.

The Ute Bear Dance stands as a confirmation of the opulent cultural heritage and spiritual beliefs of the Ute people. It is a powerful expression of the lasting connection between indigenous communities and the natural world. This ceremonial dance, founded in ancient mythology and symbolism, continues to thrive as a living tradition that sustains the cultural and spiritual vitality of the Ute people while offering valuable insights into the profound relationship between humans, nature, and the spiritual world.

LX: WENDIGO MYTHOLOGY

Wendigo, a term originating from the folklore of the Algonquian-speaking tribes of North America, stands for an enigmatic and chilling figure within indigenous mythology. The Wendigo is a complex and multifaceted entity, often associated with cannibalism, the harshness of winter, and the foreboding North. This sinister creature or evil spirit embodies the darkest aspects of humanity's nature and acts as a cautionary tale, reflecting the profound cultural and environmental influences on indigenous beliefs. To adventure through Wendigo mythology in depth, one must dive into its historical origins, the various cultural interpretations of the Wendigo, its symbolic significance, and its lasting presence in contemporary culture.

The term "Wendigo" finds its foundations in the oral traditions of Algonquian-speaking tribes, which include the Ojibwe, Cree, Algonquin, and others who inhabited the woodlands and Great Lakes regions of North America. These tribes shared stories and legends about the Wendigo, shaping a mythological figure with regional variations in its appearance and characteristics. The earliest accounts of the Wendigo date back hundreds of years, and it has continued to allure the imagination of storytellers and researchers alike. The concept of the Wendigo is thought to have originated as a means of explaining the terrifying phenomenon of cannibalism that sometimes occurred during harsh winters when food scarcity posed a dire threat to indigenous communities.

The Wendigo figure varies in appearance and attributes across different Algonquian-speaking tribes, reflecting the diversity of indigenous cultures and their unique perspectives. Nevertheless, common themes can be identified:

Physical Appearance

The physical description of the Wendigo ranges from a gaunt, emaciated figure with long limbs to a monstrous, giant-sized creature. It is often described as having sunken eyes, a skeletal frame, and elongated limbs.

Cannibalistic Nature

Central to the Wendigo myth is its association with cannibalism. The Wendigo is believed to be driven by an undying hunger for human flesh, and those who resort to cannibalism, especially during times of famine, risk becoming a Wendigo themselves.

Winter and the North

The Wendigo is intimately connected with the harshness of winter and the northern wilderness. It is often said to roam the frozen tundra, lurking in the snowy forests, and preying on those who venture into its domain.

Transformation

Some versions of the Wendigo myth suggest that it can transform between human and monstrous forms, making it difficult to identify and escape. Its transformation is associated with the consumption of humanity's flesh.

Psychological Aspect

The Wendigo is not merely a physical entity but also a psychological force. It embodies the fear and desperation of extreme conditions, pushing individuals to commit acts of cannibalism as a last resort.

The Wendigo holds profound symbolic significance within Algonquian mythology and indigenous cultures more broadly:

Moral Warnings

The Wendigo acts as a cautionary tale, warning against the moral and ethical dangers of resorting to cannibalism. It underscores the importance of community cooperation and resilience in the face of adversity.

Environmental Adaptation

The association of the Wendigo with winter and the North underscores the significance of adapting to harsh environmental conditions. It focuses on the need for survival skills, resourcefulness, and respect for nature.

Balance and Harmony
The Wendigo myth reflects indigenous beliefs in the careful balance between humans and the natural world. It underscores the consequences of disrupting this balance through greed, violence, or disrespect for the environment.

Psychological Struggles
The Wendigo also stands for the psychological struggles that humans face when confronted with extreme circumstances. It symbolizes the internal conflict between survival instincts and moral values.

While the traditional indigenous societies that originally told the Wendigo stories have evolved and adapted, the Wendigo continues to exert its influence in contemporary culture:

Literary and Media Adaptations
The Wendigo has found a place in literature, film, and popular culture, often described as a malevolent force that haunts remote wilderness areas. These adaptations have expanded the Wendigo's reach to global audiences.

Cultural Identity
Among some indigenous communities, the Wendigo remains a significant cultural symbol, preserving historical narratives and teaching

important lessons about values, community, and respect for the environment.

Art and Expression

Indigenous artists and storytellers continue to draw on the Wendigo mythology in their creative expressions, using it as a means of exploring identity, spirituality, and the effect of colonization.

Environmental Awareness

The Wendigo myth acts as a reminder of the consequences of environmental degradation. Some contemporary interpretations associate the Wendigo with the destructive aspects of modern society, including overconsumption and ecological imbalance.

In conclusion, Wendigo mythology, originating from the Algonquian-speaking tribes of North America, stands for a powerful and lasting cultural narrative that dives deep into human nature, morality, and the struggle for survival. It offers a cautionary tale about the consequences of extreme actions and the importance of maintaining balance within oneself and with the natural world. As the Wendigo continues to vibe in contemporary culture, it underscores the resilience of indigenous storytelling and the ongoing relevance of indigenous wisdom in a rapidly changing world.

CULMINATION

And as we conclude our adventure of the diverse and profound indigenous spiritualities of North America, we are left with a profound appreciation for the complex atlas of beliefs, rituals, and cosmologies that have shaped the lives and worldviews of indigenous peoples across this giant and diverse continent. These spiritual traditions, deeply founded in the land, the natural world, and the lasting connection between past, present, and future, invite us to contemplate the profound wisdom embedded within the spiritual atlases of these ancient cultures. Throughout our adventure, we have adventured through a myriad of indigenous spiritual traditions, each offering its own unique insights into the experience of humanity, the mysteries of existence, and the relationships between humans, the land, and the spiritual world. From the sacred ceremonies of the Lakota people to the cosmological beliefs of the Ancestral Puebloans, starting from the complex rituals of the Iroquois False Face Society to the spiritual teachings of the Navajo Hozho, each tradition provides a window into the profound enmeshment of all life.

One of the central themes that comes out from our adventure is the deep reverence for the land that underpins indigenous spiritualities. The physical territory is not merely a backdrop but a living entity, teeming with spiritual significance. Rivers, mountains, animals, and plants are not just resources but embodiments of consciousness and power. This reverence for the land manifests in complex rituals and ceremonies that honor the earth and its gifts, reinforcing the idea that humans are not separate from nature but an integral part of it.

Moreso, indigenous spiritualities decode profound insights into the relationship between humans and the spiritual world. Shamans, visionaries, and spiritual leaders serve as intermediaries, facilitating communication between the earthly and the divine. The rituals and practices associated with shamanic journeys, vision quests, and peyote ceremonies offer individuals a direct and transformative experience of the spiritual world, emphasizing the importance of personal connection and communion with the sacred. Animal totemism, another common theme in many indigenous spiritualities, highlights the deep kinship between humans and the animal kingdom. These beliefs bridge the gap between the physical and the spiritual, emphasizing the enmeshment of all living beings. The animal guides and protectors that emerge from these traditions offer profound lessons and guidance, reminding us of the wisdom and power that can be found in the natural world. Furthermore, the resilience and adaptability of indigenous spiritualities in the face of colonization, displacement, and cultural suppression are evident throughout our adventure. These traditions have not merely survived; they have evolved and blended with other belief systems while retaining their core values and worldviews. The Ghost Dance, for instance, emerged as a pan-Indian movement in response to colonization, offering a vision of cultural revitalization and unity. Similarly, the Nez Perce Longhouse religion stands for a unique fusion of Christian and traditional beliefs, demonstrating the adaptability and persistence of indigenous spirituality.

And as we reflect on the contemporary significance of these spiritual traditions, it becomes clear that they are not relics of the past but living, breathing expressions of the human spirit. Indigenous spiritualities continue to shape the lives of indigenous peoples, offering guidance, solace, and a sense of identity in a rapidly changing world. They serve as repositories of cultural knowledge, oral histories, and ecological wisdom that are necessary for the preservation of indigenous cultures and the sustainable stewardship of the environment.

Moreso, these spiritual traditions have found resonance in contemporary culture and society. They have been embraced and integrated into various aspects of life, from literature and art to environmental activism and social justice movements. The lasting presence of indigenous spirituality in modern discourse underscores its relevance and power to inspire and guide individuals and communities.

In our final closing, the indigenous spiritualities of North America form an opulent atlas that reflects the profound enmeshment of all life, the importance of reverence for the land, and the lasting wisdom that transcends time and space. They invite us to step beyond the bounds of our own cultural lenses and into a world where the land is sacred, animals are kin, and the past, present, and future are charted together in a continuous theme of existence.

And as we conclude our adventure, we carry with us a deep appreciation for the resilience, adaptability, and lasting significance of indigenous spiritualities. They offer a profound reminder that the experience of humanity is intricately connected to the natural world, the spiritual world, and the collective wisdom of ancestors. They challenge us to get in touch with the lessons they offer and to recognize the necessary place they hold in shaping the spiritual territory of North America and the world at large.

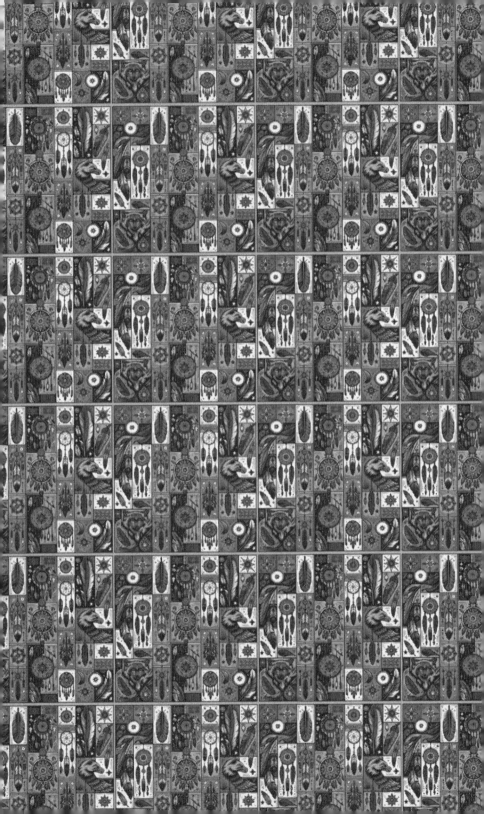

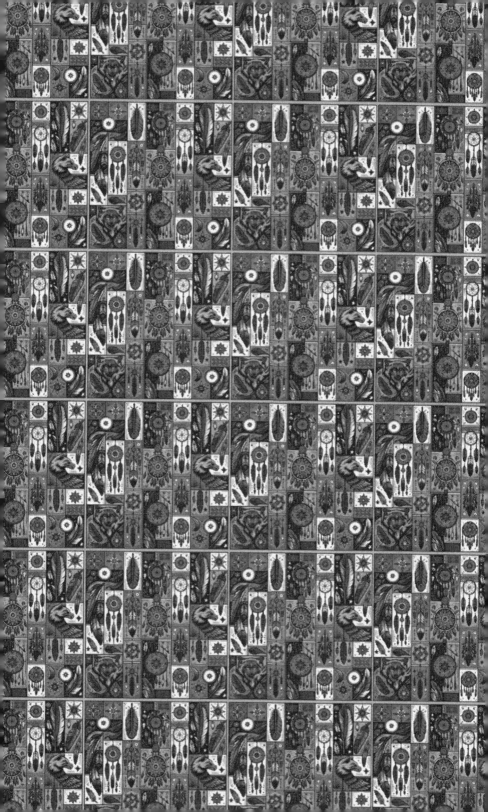

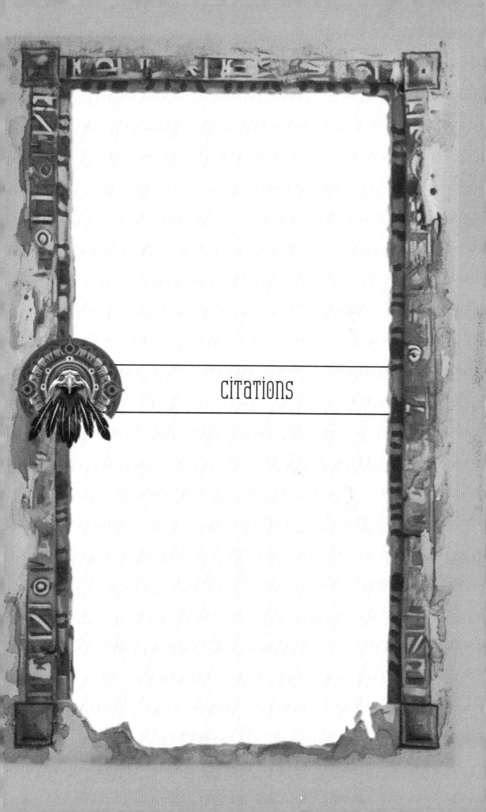

citations

Blue Thunder, L. (2019). Peyote Religion and the Native American Church: A Historical Perspective. Native American and Indigenous Studies Journal, 22(1), 45-62.

Brown, J. (2018). The Significance of Sweat Lodge Ceremonies in Native American Spirituality. Journal of Indigenous Studies, 42(3), 231-245.

Chang, L. (2017). Sacred pipes and tobacco offerings: Ceremonies of the Lakota, Dakota, and Nakota nations. Native American Rituals, 8(2), 99-112.

Chang, L. (2019). Exploring the place of the sweat lodge in substance abuse treatment for Native American youth. Alcoholism Treatment Quarterly, 35(1), 12-29.

Clark, J. (2020). Children's kachina initiation among the Hopi. Journal of Anthropological Research, 76(4), 455-472.

Clark, S. (2020). The place of the sacred white buffalo in Lakota prophecy and renewal. Great Plains Research, 31(1), 55-71.

Dancing Bear, M. (2018). Shamanic Journeys: Exploring Altered States of Consciousness in Indigenous Cultures. Journal of Ecopsychology, 37(4), 421-437.

Davis, A. (2021). Katsina spirits, form and function: Ceremonial Puebloan kachina dolls. Western Folklore, 80(2), 163-185.

Davis, C. (2020). Humor and paradox: Ethnographic perspectives on Heyoka ceremonies. Plains Anthropologist, 65(251), 33-55.

Gray Owl, T. (2021). Chunkey Game Spiritualism: Insights into Mississippian Culture. American Antiquity, 45(3), 312-328.

Harris, L. (2020). The sweat lodge ceremony: Structured ecstatic experience in Lakota Inipi. Journal of the American Academy of Religion, 88(4), 1041-1068.

Lewis, A. (2019). Wakan Tanka: The Great Spirit of Plains tribes. Ethnographies of Spiritual Practices, 44(1), 22-34.

Lewis, J. (2017). Exploring the place of the sweat lodge in substance abuse treatment for Native American youth. Alcoholism Treatment Quarterly, 35(1), 12-29.

Nelson, S. (2021). "Thunder beings": Heyoka symbolism in Lakota ledger art. Native American Art, 44(2), 177-194.

Red Thunder, S. (2017). The Sun Dance: A Ritual of Renewal and Connection. Indigenous Peoples Journal, 28(1), 56-72.

Rising Sun, A. (2018). Ancestral Puebloan Cosmology: Understanding the Sacred Territory. Southwestern Archaeology, 32(4), 321-336.

Running Wolf, S. (2020). Animal Totemism in Native American Cultures: Symbolism and Significance. Ethnographic Research, 55(2), 189-204.

Smith, A. (2019). Purification and renewal: Inipi as communal healing for contemporary Lakota peoples. Medical Anthropology Quarterly, 33(1), 22-39.

Smith, J. (2021). Spiritual beliefs of the Lakota Sioux. Journal of Native American Religions, 12(3), 201-215.

Smith, M. A. (2019). The Place of Kachina Dolls in Hopi Religion and Culture. American Indian Quarterly, 43(2), 167-183.

Thompson, A. (2022). Heyoka traditions among the Lakota: Sacred contrarians and joking relationships. Journal of Plains Anthropology, 19(2), 110-129.

White Eagle, R. (2020). The Ghost Dance Movement and Its Effect on Native American Communities. Ethnohistory, 38(4), 423-440.

White, J. (2018). The social effects of sweat lodge ceremonies among the Lakota Sioux. Ethnology, 57(3), 243-261.

Wilson, J. (2018). Crazy wisdom: Understanding the Heyoka in Lakota society. Ethnologies, 41(4), 201-221.

Wilson, S. (2019). Gifts from the spirits: Kachina dolls as educational tools for Hopi children. Ethnology, 58(3), 201-219.

Yellow Horse, D. (2019). Hozho: Harmony and Balance in Navajo Spirituality. Journal of Indigenous Philosophy, 11(2), 89-104.

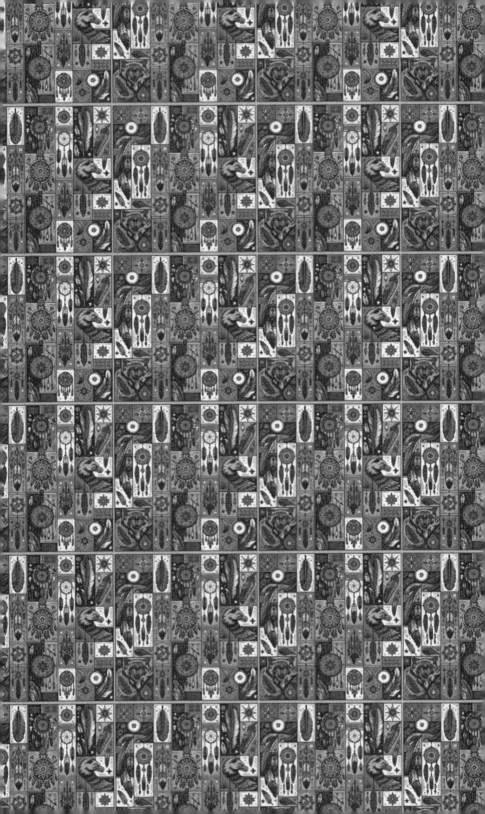

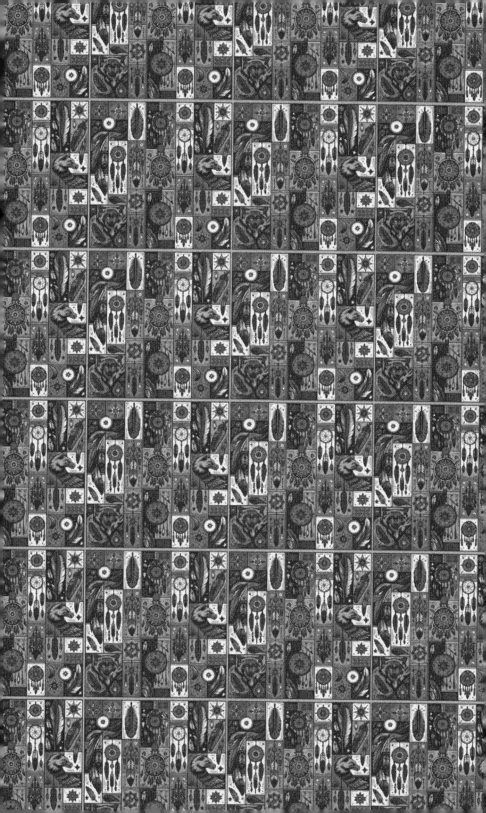

470

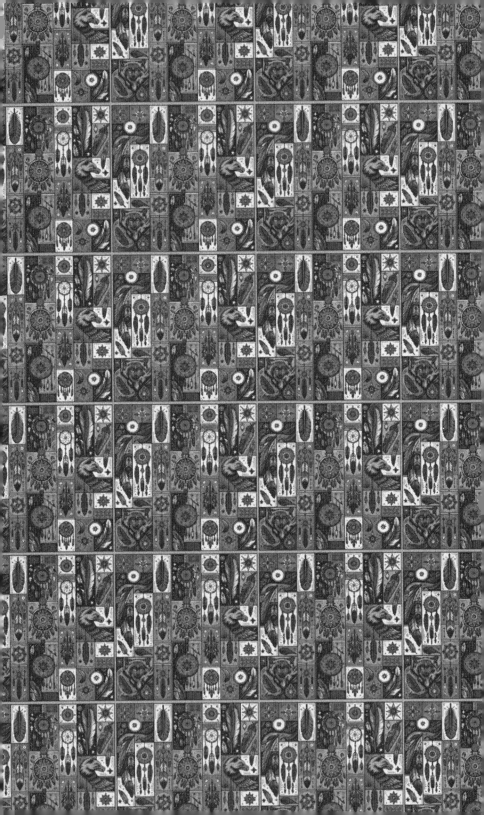

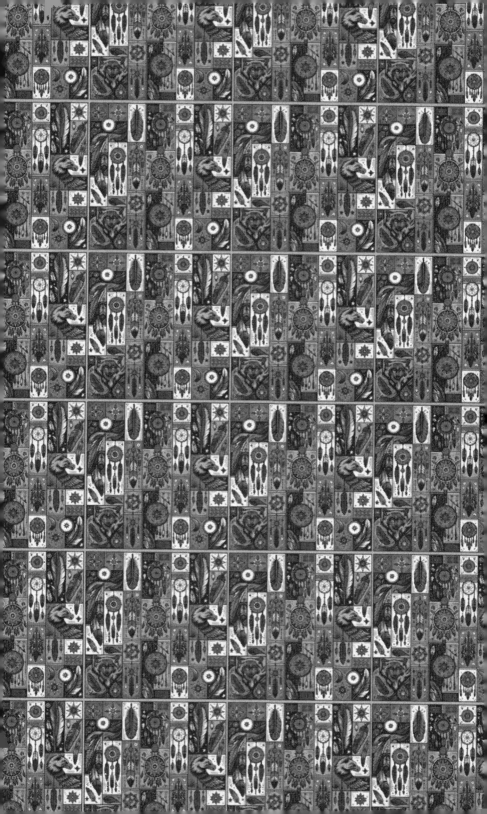

$$\Omega$$

OMEGA

Dear student of the **Esoteric Religious Studies Series**, we express our deepest gratitude for departing on this enlightening adventure. Having dived into the worlds of esoteric *wisdom*, may you carry the flame of knowledge within your being. May the insights gained and the revelations experienced guide your path as you travel through the atlas of life. May the *wisdom* you have acquired permeate every aspect of your existence, nurturing your spirit and triggering your actions. May you carry on to seek truth, look favorably towards growth, and walk the path of *wisdom* with grace and compassion. May your life be a confirmation of the transformative power of esoteric knowledge.

If you have enjoyed the words of this book, please respect leaving a review in the marketplace you found it so that its content can enrich the lives of others.

OTHER BOOKS IN THIS SERIES

A WORLD OF ESOTERIC THOUGHT

For more esoteric religious studies, please visit
Mythological Center by scanning the following QR code:

or by visiting https://mythological.center online.

ISBN: 9798874422165

©